THE STRANGER WITHIN

THE STRANGER WITHIN

The Discovery of the Inner Self

by

CYRIL H. POWELL

M.Litt., Ph.D.

*On the way home that evening, I decided that
I would call the stranger within me the Helper.*

JULIAN DUGUID.

EVESHAM

Published by
ARTHUR JAMES LIMITED
THE DRIFT, EVESHAM, WORCS.

First published — 1962

© — Arthur James Ltd. — 1962

MADE AND PRINTED IN GREAT BRITAIN BY PURNELL AND SONS, LTD.
PAULTON (SOMERSET) AND LONDON

DEDICATION

To those who, over the years,
have helped me towards this
discovery.

Words of Welcome

from

Hugh Redwood

I WELCOME Dr. Cyril Powell's book because I believe that through reading it, many will come to understand better the "Kingdom within" of which Jesus Christ spoke.

It is a book of true Christian psychology: a deep book, but deeply refreshing. It goes to the roots, in the inner self, of the evils by which our world is so frighteningly beset, and in that very place shows us deliverance and the Deliverer; the reality of re-creation, and the transformation of personality through the life of Christ indwelling.

As with Dr. Powell's previous book, his new book is something which people should read, study and then pass to another. I do, indeed, warmly welcome this book.

Orpington,   HUGH REDWOOD
Kent.

CONTENTS

9

CONTENTS

Part I

Discovery

Thou desirest truth in the inward parts: and in the hidden part thou shalt make me to know wisdom.

PSALM 51.

Look Within!

The Kingdom of God is within you.[1]

JESUS

THERE is urgent need for frank Christian appraisal of factors which others in our day are exploiting. Some of us have been more than a little surprised at the admissions made recently by certain advertising specialists. "We are all depth boys now," is the way one executive expressed this. He meant that their publicity campaigns were geared to facts revealed by "depth psychology".

It is obvious to anyone who studies the human scene carefully that there are factors working deeper in our minds than just our powers of calm reason and honest logic. We can observe human beings exhibiting irrational prejudices, favouring certain things without knowing why, and being instinctively "drawn" to certain people while reacting from others.

What has Christianity to say concerning these hidden forces operating within every one of us? How can we guard against their exploitation? How can we be sure that *this* part of our nature shall express itself to the glory of God?

There is abundant need for investigation here.

In these past months much previous thinking and experience have crystallized for me. It began when some readers of another book of mine wrote regarding some of their findings. The book had discussed some of the problems connected with loneliness. One or two of the letters distinguished between empty and desolating loneliness and the deliberate seeking of a form of solitude that had nothing but the most beneficial results.

"I have found a way of being alone," one man reported, "that is the opposite of lonely. I value my solitary moments. They are my times of communion with God."

"The fact is," commented another, "we need to seek solitude in order to break away from enslavement to the mass society of our day. Because they don't take time and trouble to be alone so many people just absorb the notions that are abroad. Their minds aren't their own. I need solitude in order to find, and keep, my soul."

These letters were from folk who had discovered one of life's greatest secrets. But I also heard from others, equally anxious to find an answer to their difficulties, who could not understand how time spent in solitude could be anything but an empty horror.

What, I began asking myself, were the writers of these letters inviting me to explore? The challenge proved to be complementary to that coming from the "depth boys" of modern advertising. The difference between the first and second group of correspondents concerned a level of life where the distress of loneliness receives its final solution, not through exploitation, but through fulfilment of underlying forces. My problem was to show this second group of anxious, seeking writers where the answer lay, and to introduce them to the Stranger Within so that he should be a stranger no more.

Up to the age of about forty, life has a way of carrying most of us forward in a steady momentum. Only the lonely and the introspective find it otherwise. We are engrossed in the processes of growing up, marrying, establishing a home, energetically pursuing a career. All our powers and interests are engaged.

Once this mid-point at about forty is reached, however, life settles into a new rhythm. Pressing questions about the future begin to assert themselves. There is time to widen our cultural interests and to enquire how we fit into life's kaleidoscopic pattern. Pausing to analyse themselves, many find they are looking within, and for the first time come face to face with the Stranger Within.

To anybody, whatever his or her age, who has learnt to distinguish between negative and positive solitude, this discovery has already dawned, for the communion that opens up in solitude *must* come from within.

Those who shun the negative form are right, for it is a dreary emptiness lacking human companionship and the stimulus provided by our fellows. Positive solitude, on the other hand, is time deliberately taken apart from others that we might begin to know ourselves and gain inner communion with what lies at the heart of things. In his monumental *Study of History* Arnold Toynbee shows the great leaders of mankind doing this. He educes what he calls the principle of "withdrawal and return". Moses, Paul and our Lord all withdrew into the desert before they began their great work. Many other leaders have acted similarly. The withdrawal, as Toynbee says, "makes it possible for the personality to realise powers within himself which might have remained dormant if he had not been released for the time being from his social toils and trammels."[2] Equipped with new vision and power he can now return to the world in order to do his creative work.

This establishes the fact that there is a way of cultivating solitude not for escape, but for re-creation: not to "get away from people", but to be alone long enough to be able to serve them better.

In solitude there is something in us which has a chance to develop. Said André Gide, if you never find yourself alone, you will never find yourself at all.

As a result of this renewed thinking about the Stranger Within, I began sharing some of these discoveries and rediscoveries with a small group, some of whom were active Christian workers. "These facts need to be widely known," one of them said emphatically after one of our sessions. That phrase, "need to be widely known," continued to ring in my ears. It provided the genesis of this book.

After much deliberation I decided to call this inner part of our nature "The Stranger Within". Most people live in ignorance of his existence and of his power for good and ill. Do you remember our Lord's one-sentence story of the man who, working in his field with hoe or mattock, bumped into buried treasure? Could it be that our Lord had *this* idea in mind when He uttered His parable? It is certainly true that many make this discovery in the course of going about their daily life. Something is there, hidden, right in the field of our ordinary existence. To possess it is worth almost everything. By means of it we can take the way forward into life and to fellowship with God in His kingdom.

This metaphor serves to indicate how we shall regard the Stranger Within : as treasure, leading to fulness of life. Though I have spoken of the way in which this realm is exploited by others, our method here will be to suggest ways of positive co-operation with these inward forces rather than issuing warnings against their misuse. The finest safeguard is to discover how best to employ these powers for God and according to His intention. What is to be avoided is to offer the enemies of the soul an empty space, swept and garnished. If so, then seven teams of exploiters, each worse than the first, will soon be competing for ground floor positions on this vacant lot!

Nor, since our theme is the "inner self", should anyone imagine that in these pages we shall be encouraging one another to an orgy of introspection or morbid self-interest. That is not my purpose at all. This treasure has not been discovered in order to be ceaselessly fidgeting with the lock, and peering in at the open lid. What this book *is* designed to do is to help us to acknowledge the existence of the inner self, and then co-operate with it. Thus comes harmony and integration.

We can then go forward in a manner which is not only self-forgetting, but "inner-self forgetting" too. Just as in a condition of health and vigour we are not aware of the body, so we can forget our inner being. We become conscious of the body only when we slip into illness. Similarly we become preoccupied with the inner self when all is not well within. We are rightly more than a little shy of people who are always thinking and talking about their soul, and who are prepared to discuss the deeper levels of the self and lay them bare before us. This book is not addressed to that type of person, for he is suffering from a perverted form of egotism and needs help of another kind. I am concerned with the earnest seeker.

There is another important fact to remember. Living in this present era we are privileged people. Not only are the knowledge and experience of the centuries our heritage, but we live in days when the inner resources of the mind have been investigated as never before. These are the very researches upon which the motivational advertisers have been fastening. Many of the things of which we speak were known, however, to the wise of previous generations, though perhaps their way of describing them differs.

Listen for example to Marcus Aurelius, the pagan Emperor of Rome, writing in the second century. "Whenever you choose you can retire into yourself. Nowhere can a man find a retreat more peaceful or more untroubled than within his own soul." It was he also who wrote, "Look within! Within is the fountain of good, and it is always ready to bubble up, if you will always dig."

And could this from Marcus Aurelius be better stated today by the motivation engineers and analysts of whom Vance Packard tells us in *The Hidden Persuaders*? "Remember that what pulls the strings is the force hidden within: this is what lies behind our ability to persuade others, this, indeed, is our life—if one must speak plainly, this is the real man."[3]

There have been those who have settled the nature of the real "I", the Stranger Within, with too great exactitude. They have done this, at times, in very peremptory fashion. The Behaviourist is very definite about it—he dismisses the idea, as a separate concept, from the start. The inner self is something, he declares, located in the cells of the body: and in this too close identification he is wrong. "We need nothing," said Dr. J. B. Watson, the founder of Behaviourism, "to explain human behaviour but the ordinary laws of physics and chemistry." But all the parts of our bodies have been renewed many times ever since we were born. No cell that was part of us then is with us now. My brain, being part of my body, is not the same cluster of cells with which I started. But my inner self has survived all these changes.

Others have given the inner self such labels as "the unconscious mind", "the soul", the *anima*, the *ego*, the "superself". Various psychological systems have endeavoured to isolate it in this way. There was a school of thought which for a time imagined it had determined the exact spot from which the inner self operates. It was, they said, the Pineal Gland. This was ingenious for no one so far had discovered the real function of this small reddish gland situated behind the third ventricle of the brain. But it is not to be pinned down in that fashion.

When we turn inwards we find behind all our actions a vast reservoir of thought and feeling. It works through the brain, but it is not to be identified with it, nor with the other parts of the body associated with thinking and feeling, as, for example, the spinal cord or the solar plexus. It is behind all these things—a spiritual entity: our "inner self", energiser of our bodies, director of our actions, source of our unconsidered responses.

It is this that regulates the life of the body, keeps the heart beating and the lungs breathing, that looks after the body's glandular interchange, that manages us while we sleep, and has been behind all the wonder of growth. We have not had to think about, nor consciously engineer, any of these processes.

This inner self is "myself" at a deeper level than the "I" which is apparently in charge through my waking hours. My conscious self I know very well. It is that part of me that seems so much in control. By means of it I am aware of myself and others; I think; I reason; I plan. I need no one to point out to me the existence of this part of my nature. It is the inner self, by contrast, that is the Stranger whom so many do not know and of whom they take so little account.

We go forward to investigate these possibilities and to see how, in the Christian context, we are encouraged to claim much that ordinarily goes unregarded.

First, of course, we must be convinced about the existence of "The Stranger Within". In the opening chapters I shall be attempting to assemble some of the evidence coming from various directions that will enable us to identify him and understand him better. Only after this necessary preliminary investigation can we pass, as we do in Part II, to considering our full co-operation with these inner forces.

I believe that thus we shall find we are fitting ourselves in the best possible fashion to meet the challenges of the days in which we live. Up till now the earth has been the cradle of man's development. Having rocketed into space, it is time both physically and mentally for him to step out of the cradle. The first stage is for man to understand himself. The search must start from within so that he may know his real nature.

At every level we must learn how to shoulder our responsibilities. The discovery of the inner self, and coming into harmony with all to which it introduces us, is the key to fulness of living, to control of the world and its advancement, and the right use of the powers put into our hands in this atomic-and-space era at whose portals we now stand.

2

Alarm Bells

> ... We are here as on a darkling plain
> Swept with confused alarms of struggle and flight
> Where ignorant armies clash by night.
>
> MATTHEW ARNOLD[1]

BY looking at the world we discover the significance of what we are seeking. We come, indeed, to the startling conclusion that world-scale problems have to do with factors emanating from the inner selves of masses of people, and that their solution concerns the right treatment and evaluation of man's inner life.

Listen to some of the alarm bells ringing throughout the world. They warn not only of immediate action necessary to deal with society's bandits and burglars, but bid us look at the origin of these troubles and there seek for final remedies.

There can be no doubt where the loudest of these alarms is sounding: the threat of annihilation hangs over the world in the shape of atomic weapons of destruction. We need the ability to control the power now placed in the hands of man. We need world peace.

Pierre Lecomte du Noüy is an internationally known scientist. At one time he studied with Pierre and Marie Curie; he served as a doctor in the French army in the first world war. In 1917 he successfully introduced mathematics into the biological problem concerning the rate of healing of a surface wound. His concept of Biological Time, and a number of other theories and discoveries, have had their effect not only in hospitals and laboratories but also amongst philosophers throughout the world. In 1947 he produced a book born out of his concern that science, which has been used to "sap the base of religion", should now be used to consolidate it. He was anxious that man, amidst all the forces of modern materialism, should remember his fundamentally spiritual nature and safeguard for himself the things which really characterize him as man.

Towards the end of his study[2] Dr. du Noüy writes of the achievement of peace. His knowledge of the international scene, of life on the Continent and in the United States, his experiences in occupied France under the Nazis, afford a unique background for assessing the situation. It is plain that du Noüy sees no hope in efforts made at the circumference of the problem. The hope lies in dealing with it at the centre. Not in the United Nations, nor its forerunner, the League of Nations, nor in treaties or alliances is peace to be established. "The time has come for nations, as well as individuals to know what they want," he declares. "If civilized countries *want* peace, they must understand that the problem must be approached basically. The old scaffolding willed to us by past generations cracks on every side. It cannot be consolidated by make-shifts, by bits of string, by pots of glue and treaties signed by Highly-Dignified-Gentlemen. . . . Peace must be established by transforming man from the interior and not by erecting external structures. We have already said it: the source of all wars, the source of all evil, lies in us. No outside protection will be efficient if the enemy cowering at the bottom of our hearts is authorized to live."[3]

Dr. du Noüy traces the source of our troubles to fears, greeds and suspicions deep in men's minds. Some of these lie deeper than we know. The point is made that *here*, within the heart and mind of man, are the roots of what builds up into war. And for peace firmly to be established it is here that the true solution must be found. When, in these days, we have to deal with the greed of newly-formed nations we must remember that we are observing a mass outworking of the avariciousness of man.

We are not concerned at the moment with du Noüy's positive suggestions, though they are worthy of the greatest consideration. A preliminary step, he says, is that history shall be taught to the youth of all nations on a universally accurate, and not a nationally-biased basis. At the very source man's instincts must be controlled and directed, and everywhere the cult of individual human dignity preached and established.

Our concern is that, as this alarm bell of strife sounds across the world, men may hear in its tones a call not so much to increase armies, strengthen United Nations, enter into alliances and treaties, as to deal with the forces within man. This alarm peals in order to remind us of the Stranger Within—the forgotten factor that in this situation, as in all others, is of highest importance.

This distinguished scientist is anxious to reverse the forces of materialism, and to remind modern man of science's true place. It exists not to dethrone, but to exalt, man's dignity. It should be used to foster, not destroy, the spiritual side of his being.

How is this to be done? And what has gone wrong, and where has it gone wrong? Vast areas of the world are now given over to the forces of materialism, and the atmosphere of the western societies is heavily laden with the same poison. The answer again is not to be found on the surface of life, but beneath it. The masses of men have not thought about this issue. They have absorbed a superficial culture and become soaked in ideas disseminated by the leaders of a past generation.

The popular mind absorbs the pronouncements of the pundits and follows them by a margin of something like twenty-five years. In this new era of increased powers of communication, radio, press and television, and of universal education, the margin is possibly less. But the time lag is still conditioned not so much by methods of communication as by the time needed for seed ideas to establish themselves in the "unconscious minds" of a generation. The masses are now the inheritors of the thinking of Darwin and Huxley, of Marx and Engels. What was said in the laboratories and the lecture-rooms just after and about their time has percolated through to them and helped to mould their basic conceptions.

It is plain fact that the thinking of many scientists today is far more after the order of Lecomte du Noüy: but the popular mind has not yet caught up with this new, more "spiritual" emphasis. The rationalism of fifty to a hundred years ago is dead. Men no longer reason after that fashion. The fact that the atom, the final point of indestructible matter, has itself now been exploded is symptomatic of a change in the scientific thinking of our time.

As we pause to listen, other alarm bells are ringing in connection with present-day civilization. We are becoming conformists to a most distressing degree. What Big Brother says, we do. In particular the methods, aims, ethics and atmosphere of big-business engulfs everybody engaged in it—both employers and employees. The universal model is that of the conformist, the Organisation Man.[4]

After several years of research by a small group under the sponsorship of the Yale University Commission on National Policy, David Riesman wrote *The Lonely Crowd*. Its thesis is that a change has taken place in the character of the American people from "inner direction" to "other direction". (Riesman could have called the latter "outer direction" and still have been right!) By this is meant a change from the pioneer spirit to that of the conformist. Pioneer Americans possessed an internal authority. They were individualists, making firm decisions. Their successors are folk influenced by the example of their peers and

24

contemporaries, needing the constant approval of others. The second generation in pioneer Israel is showing the same marks of conformity. Here yet another alarm bell is ringing. The "other-directed person" is incapable of making decisions. When group pressures and stimulations from outside are taken away he is without resources. America, says Riesman, is fast becoming an "other-directed" society.

To be alone is a fate most to be dreaded by the "other-directed" man. The creative process of withdrawal and return, of which Arnold Toynbee writes, is unknown to him. So far from solitude being at times something to be sought after, it becomes the state most to be shunned.

What we are witnessing in our city life and our big-business organisation is the outworking of the powerful forces of mass suggestion and daily routine. These *do* something to our personalities: and the point at which the damage is done is within.

The hopeful signs are the very occurrences that occasionally disturb us: the teenage rebellions and the assertions of independence that at times seem little more successful than Sancho Panza's tilting at windmills.

The very rumbles of discontent and dissatisfaction may prove to be the tuning-up in the future symphony of hope. If people, without any signs of revolt, proved amenable to all the aspects of mass living they would have to be labelled as less than human. The 1956 rising in Hungary was one such eruption of the human spirit. Men and women could stand their enforced slavery no longer.

It is sometimes possible to learn at first-hand about this kind of rebellion breaking out under totalitarian rule. Just before Christmas 1960, I was a member of a small deputation that went to Berlin to talk with some of the Protestant pastors and leaders from the East Zone of Germany. We heard of their trials and difficulties under Communist rule, and marvelled at their strength and patience, and at what

God was doing amongst them and their people. One of the things we heard concerned some youths in a big city in the heart of the East Zone. One Saturday a group of them did something to which the People's Police objected, and the latter took a somewhat high-handed attitude. The youths resented this, and within minutes a crowd of youngsters gathered. In a short time there must have been something like a thousand of them in the area. It was all spontaneous. There is no chance of organising anything like this in Communist countries. The youths began picking up paving-stones and throwing them at the police. They overturned their van. Reinforcements speedily arrived, and the crowd in the square was surrounded and then dealt with. This had happened in the summer, and when we met in December some of those youths were still in prison. The point about this story is that many of them were sons of communist functionaries. Though brought up in the system and indoctrinated in it from earliest days there came a time when with the unpredictable compulsion of youth they inwardly rebelled, fully aware of what would happen if they took outward action.

About Moscow Communism, one German leader said, "If this system cracks, it will not be because it is anti-Christian, but because it is against human nature." I know what he meant, though I would have expressed it differently, for I believe that what is against human nature is at the same time anti-Christian. Man is born to be free, and the place where this freedom originates and exercises its force is in the centre of his being. Whenever men rebel against tyranny and authoritarian rule, the Stranger Within is declaring himself. Part of the glory of the Christian faith is expressed in the phrase concerning God from a collect in the Book of Common Prayer, "whose service is perfect freedom".

In all manner of differing circumstances we can detect what is often worthy to be called a "divine discontent".

Its manifestation at times may be anything but divine, but the stirrings deep within have their connection with divinity. Many living under Communism, and others living in the "affluent society" of America, or secure in Britain under the provisions of the Welfare State, are not content. They are in a far country, and know something of how the Prodigal felt when he would fain have filled his belly with the husks that the swine did eat, and no man gave unto him.

Notice too, other forms in which the Stranger is announcing himself. These have to do with our private rather than our public lives. Yet they equally concern everybody.

One form that the announcement takes is the universal longing for a fuller, more integrated life. We want "all our soul's and body's powers" to be at one: but even whilst we feel this longing we do not realise how deep we have to go within our nature to answer it. Since the Stranger Within is either largely unknown or actively resented, this universal longing for integration is not usually expressed very intelligently nor is it likely of fulfilment. But its very existence is a pointer to these unknown depths within.

Then the almost universal desire for communion with God is another indication of the existence of the realm within, for this is where this fellowship opens.

Cleopatra's words in Shakespeare's play are often quoted, "I have immortal longings in me". So have we all, in deeper ways than perhaps Cleopatra meant, and these are indications, again, of the Stranger. These intimations of, and longings for, immortality have both their origin and their reason for existing here. It is *this* part of our nature that continues beyond bodily death. All else we leave behind. It is our "self" that goes forward naked into the hereafter. This is why, if when we come to pass into that new stage our real self is poor and undeveloped, we enter it hopelessly ill-prepared.

Earlier in this chapter we spoke of the ray of hope shining amid the democratization, the levelling out process, of modern life, when someone's spirit rises in discontent and rebellion. The process may be uncomfortable, but it witnesses to the existence of the inner life. From this centre the unexpected and the unpredictable continue to break out, for we are men not automata. Within man is a fund of creativity, of inner direction. And it is from this point that each of God's children can grow according to his own stamp and measure, not according to a pattern forced on him by society from without. This is the source of hope.

The individual is bound to be influenced by his environment, but he must learn how to withstand its pressures. The key to this is in the realm within. Often it is because of the pain caused by these tensions that we become aware of the Stranger Within. We can thus learn a new philosophy concerning some of our distress. The pain we sometimes feel is a token of the Stranger's existence. If we begin to take account of what he would say to us, there are great possibilities ahead.

Take comfort in your loneliness and anxiety if at the moment you are acutely conscious of them. Interpreted rightly, they afford promise that the future can be quite different. These present stresses imply dis-ease which can pass, giving way to peace and harmony. It is so for the individual, and it can be so for man in society.

So listen and heed when the alarm bells begin to ring. They are calling us to take notice of these deeper, forgotten factors. And as, from day to day, we feel the challenge of world problems and world issues we can learn how best to see into them and answer them. Many of these complex problems should first be broken down to the scale of the individual. On that level they can be grasped and understood. When their direct relationship to individuals is realised many complicated issues become clarified. Not until we grapple with the inner self will some of the most persistent world problems be solved. Through the pages of this book we shall be exploring the inner life of individuals, and for that reason we shall not be far away from the most urgent and tremendous issues of our day.

3

The Seed-Bed of Personality

And we will walk the weeded field
And tell the golden harvest's yield.

JOHN MASEFIELD[1]

WHERE do the mass suggestions of our time find a
place where they can take root and grow? Where is
it that the pressures of our surrounding civilization register
and the impulses towards conformity begin to operate?

In the previous chapter we listened to clanging warnings
inviting us to take stock of ourselves. Take care, some of
them seem to be saying, Christian democracy is in danger
of suffering severe setbacks. The under-developed countries
cannot be blamed for adopting our western ideals of freedom and justice. Through trial and error, we have found
them to be true. Today, however, we are witnessing a
strange germination from these tested seed-ideas. Some
very twisted and stunted plants seem to be emerging.
Why? Because the seeds were sown in greedy, ill-prepared
soil. It is the individual who absorbs ideas, and the pre-
ponderating voice of the mass of individuals tends to
formulate policy. Responsible statesmen are only too well
aware of this.

So if we are to silence the jangling alarm bells, we must
turn to the deep working of the personality and study the
individual Stranger Within, for it is he who accepts ideas
and then reissues them in action.

At this stage we are wise to refer to the Bible and notice
that this problem was discussed two thousand years ago.

No better introduction to this aspect of our subject can be found.

Four well-known parables refer to the evolution of seed-ideas. First there is the story of the sower and the soil; then the parable of the mustard seed, so small yet becoming a great tree; then the picture of the farmer casting seed into the ground, sleeping and rising night and day, the seed springing up and growing "he knoweth not how"; and finally, the story of the tares sown amongst the wheat.

Obviously our Lord found here a pointed description of processes going forward in human nature.

As He uses the metaphor in His teaching the seed symbolises the kingdom of God's Love and Power. It has, He says, "life in itself", increasing in good ground thirty, sixty or a hundredfold. Like mustard, it grows from something tiny into something great. There is nothing wrong with the seed. It is bound to grow, provided the conditions are right.

The variable factor is that of the soil and its potential. Normally, notice, the earth accepts indiscriminately whatever seeds fall into it, offering opportunity for germination and growth. In the parable of the tares the point is made that the seeds of evil have an equal chance to develop with the good. The soil, in itself, does not choose what it will receive. It cannot. This is exactly the case with the inner self of which the soil is the symbol.

It is important to notice another fact concerning this metaphor. In the terms of the parable of the seed growing secretly (Mark 4: 26ff), the process of growth as it goes forward is *unconscious*. The processes are beyond the farmer's understanding and his immediate control.

With this clue we can understand how men come to reap some of the harvests that are theirs in later life. They are astonished sometimes at what happens, and so are others. But they need not be. Deep impressions in childhood, powerful ideas and suggestions accepted long since, grudges and hatreds buried deep, fears never recognized —all these have been planted in the seed-bed of personality and from them a harvest is gathered.

We can notice the influence of seed-ideas at work in the lives of others. What has been said casually to impressionable people has often gone deep. Who, I wonder, cannot recall from his own experience a similar incident to this that befell Leo Tolstoy? After long separation, he met his elder brother in Paris. Occupying the same room, the elder brother was soon in bed without making any gesture of Christian devotion. Leo, watching, hesitated for a moment. Then he knelt, according to his custom. When he rose, he met the staring eyes of his brother, who said, "You still do that?" No other word was uttered. But this negative suggestion was enough. Tolstoy has left it on record that in consequence it was eighteen years before he prayed again.

Some of the most powerful seed-ideas are not recognized at the time of their arrival, nor is their source always remembered. Consequently many people have lost trace of the formative influences behind their lives. Biography is, however, full of well-remembered and well-documented instances. Albert Schweitzer, that great figure of our own time, acknowledges how much he owes to the influence of family and friends and also to chance acquaintances who, because of what they said or did "entered my life and became powers within me." "If we had before us," he comments, "those who have thus been a blessing to us and could tell them how it came about, they would be amazed to learn what passed over from their life into ours."

The Scot, Andrew Carnegie, who before he died had given away £70,000,000, was able to trace the influence that made him so fervent a patriot. Though he made his millions in America and distributed his philanthropy throughout the world, his heart was given for ever to the land of his birth, where at the age of ten he was a poor bobbin-boy in a cotton factory. For this glowing patriotism his uncle was responsible—and the hero to whom his uncle introduced him. "Uncle Lauder has told me," reported Carnegie, "that he often brought people into the room, assuring them that he could make my brother and me weep, laugh, or close our little fists, ready to fight . . . in short, play upon our moods through the influence of poetry and song. The betrayal of Wallace was his trump card, which never failed to cause our little hearts to sob, a complete breakdown being the inevitable result. . . . No matter how often he told the story, it never lost its hold. How wonderful is the influence of a hero upon children." Then the multi-millionaire adds these significant words, "If the source of that prime article—courage—were studied, I am sure the final analysis would find it founded upon Wallace, the hero of Scotland." It was from his boy-hood hero that Carnegie inherited his outstanding grit and determination.

My Scottish mother had a care for money and an instinct for thrift bred in her from earliest days. Life in a fishing village in the far north helped to inculcate a healthy respect for material things. "Take care of the pence and the pounds will take care of themselves," she used to say. I heard this so often that it became ingrained in me, until at twenty I caught myself out in an act of meanness involving the colossal sum of sixpence. When I realised the extent of my meanness, I was horrified. It was time to break with this philosophy accepted as a seed idea without realising it. Perhaps those who know me best will say that they haven't yet noticed that the results have altogether been eradicated!

Let one more instance suffice to underline the point I am making regarding seed influences. Dr. Edward C. Rosenow, famous bacteriologist of the Mayo Clinic, who did so much towards the alleviation and cure of infantile paralysis, has confided how he determined to become a doctor. It was one night when his brother was dangerously ill and the doctor came to their isolated farm in Wisconsin. No one observed the small boy who followed the rest into the sickroom, but the boy himself watched everything that happened. He particularly noticed one thing. It settled his future. After a careful, patient examination of his brother, the doctor turned to the parents and said, "Have no fear. He's going to get well." It was as if a light spread across their faces. Young Edward knew then that, more than anything else, he wanted to belong to a profession that could flood people's faces with such relief.

Seed ideas are showered on us. They fall into our lives sometimes by the merest chance. But once the seed is allowed to germinate it will spring up, grow and issue in a harvest. This is a law of life. Processes such as education and indoctrination proceed, consciously and unconsciously, on the basis of this relationship, as also the science of advertising. Education is much more than a process of introduction to knowledge, the assimilation of facts, and the learning of certain skills. Educators, whether they know it or not, affect those in their charge with seed-ideas, powerful germinating conceptions that may develop into life interests or even into life prejudices. They can stimulate their pupils to enthusiasm or cause feelings of ennui and boredom.

I have known gifted pupils, doing well at a certain subject, to be turned against it because at a crucial time they were condemned to study the subject under a new, uncongenial teacher. When dealing with those in the impressionable years of youth, the sower of seed can exercise enormous influence, knowingly or unknowingly.

It is the people and ideas, that "kindle our imagination", that have power over us and do things in us. Across the years I shall never cease to be grateful for those who first made me *feel* the worthwhileness of certain ways of life, who made something in my soul leap at the call of beauty, who fired me with the glory of words as the vehicle of glowing ideas, and helped me to know Christ.

The name of Monsieur Coué is not as well known now as it was some forty years ago, but we should still be wise to take account of some of the things this Frenchman brought to our attention. He was a great exponent of the forces of suggestion and auto-suggestion. It was he who taught his patients to say morning and evening, "Every day and in every way I am getting better and better." Of course in itself this formula is not sufficient to make a patient's health improve, but as part of a treatment it provides a very good example of the seed-idea which, once accepted by the deeper mind, has power to alter life's direction, in this case from ill-health to health. Constructive suggestion can reinforce all the other powers of the body working towards renewed health. The formula alone seems altogether too simple, almost too ridiculous a weapon with which to fight the forces of disease, but Monsieur Coué has often been proved to be a great deal wiser than his critics.

One of his statements that has survived is "when the will and the imagination are in conflict, it is the imagination that invariably wins". A plank twelve inches in width and one and a half in thickness stretched between two walls three feet from the ground is strong enough to carry a man. We know this and can walk across in certainty. Alter the distance from the ground by thirty feet, and though we know it is still the same plank, and though our reason argues it is safe, will and imagination are in conflict. Imagination is concerned with the thirty-foot drop. Crestfallen, we abandon the crossing.

If we examined the truth behind M. Coué's statement we should find that what he is really saying is that the inner self is often stronger than the outward, conscious self. With our will and our conscious thought we may direct ourselves to do certain things, yet if our imagination has set forces stirring deeper down in our nature, then these will often prove to be stronger.

Notice how skilful advertisers play upon this knowledge of seed ideas. Two things motivate them: the slogan to kindle the imagination; and the personality who will help to "sell" the product. Well-known names and well-known faces, made popular through sport, radio and television, offer the best possible backing. As these faces beam at us from the advertising strip, we are assured that they have used so-and-so's toothpaste to their everlasting advantage. Their wide display of gleaming teeth induces the unwary to imagine that he or she can rise to similar heights of pearly whiteness and thus emulate the handsomeness or beauty of their favourite movie star.[2]

As we have noted it is our Lord Himself who directs attention to this important sower-seed-soil correlation. Many are the people who stand in the capacity of sower. One of the strongest of all relationships is that between mother and child, and so many habitual ideas and strong prejudices can be traced back to what "mother said" or "mother did". At school we are greatly influenced by other children, especially the "heroes" and "heroines" whom we appoint as lords over us. What they say and do matters tremendously. Seed-ideas are being received daily from all manner of everyday sources. But few are half so powerful as those received from some T.V. star, whose mannerisms are unconsciously cultivated by thousands of admiring fans.

Later, the organisation that absorbs us has its influence; our friends; the leaders we admire. . . . It is a fascinating study to trace the source of much that issues in our conduct today. When and how was *that* seed planted? And who was the sower?

These influences are at their most potent when we are young and impressionable: but throughout life this mechanism is at work. When Francis Thompson at 21 was a medical student in Manchester, his mother gave him, without any known cause or purpose, a copy of de Quincey's *Confessions of an English Opium Eater*. It was an influence of the strongest kind. Young Thompson became a drug addict. Everard Meynell in his *Life of Francis Thompson* writes of "this momentous introduction, fraught with suggestions and sympathies for which there was a gaping readiness in the young man." "Constitutionally," comments Meynell, "he was a target for the temptation of the drug; doubly a target when set up in the mis-fitting guise of a medical student, and sent about his work in the middle of the city of Manchester, long according to de Quincey, a dingy den of opium, with every facility of access, and all the pains that were de Quincey's excuse." Then Meynell adds these dreadful words, "He took opium at the hands of de Quincey and his mother."[3]

All of us—parents, teachers, potential sowers of seed-ideas in the lives of other people—need to be more alert and aware of our grave responsibilities at these formative times.

Regarding our own lives we must remember, too, that the inner self is like productive soil, as the Parable of the Tares reminds us, not discriminating between the seeds planted in it. It is the conscious, controlling part of us that has the important task of exercising this vital responsibility. Unworthy ideas, untrue advertisements, wrong notions are to be detected by the conscious mind for what they are, and rejected immediately, no matter who is trying to implant the seed.

When we detect in ourselves, and others, the emergence of a bad harvest, we should appreciate that the blame may in part rest with a reckless sower of seed-thoughts. When once we understand the possible origin of our sins and errors we should take heart. We have grasped a principle in accordance with which our lives have been *unconsciously* working. Here is something which henceforward we can take into account. There is a guard which we can post at the door leading to the inner self. With steadfast watching and praying we can fight to strangle the evil growth and foster the good. What a glorious harvest can be brought to perfection if we will tend the seeds of the Kingdom!

Not only is all this of importance in its own right, but by this examination of the mechanism concerning "seed-ideas" we have added further evidence to our case regarding the importance and power of the forces of the inner self, the Stranger Within. When we turn to look at the allied subject of hypnosis in the next chapter we shall find that the evidence begins to be overwhelming.

4
Power Within

Man is a stream whose source is hidden. Always our being is descending into us from we know not what.

R. W. Emerson[1]

IF we are to understand ourselves fully and attain a true balance in life then the facts about the forces within us must be acknowledged, and considered in our modern setting. There is nothing novel about Hypnotism, for in varying forms it has been practised since time immemorial, but its use has been investigated and developed within recent times, especially since the days of Mesmer, and in connection with the schools of French psychological medicine. By means of what is now a well-established technique a short cut through to the inner self can be found.

Some years ago I was privileged to work with a doctor engaged in psychiatry. We shared in a number of experiences which have for ever convinced me of the immense power available to, and coming through, the inner self. In order to reach the patient at this deeper level we occasionally used hypnotism. The patient's consent was first obtained and then he or she was put into a trance-like sleep. While the "conscious" mind was thus short-circuited, being virtually asleep, the patient continued to hear the voice of the practitioner, and accepted his suggestions. We found questions could be asked of a co-operative patient under hypnosis and answers were sometimes received that were not forthcoming from his normal conscious self.

Commands and suggestions were made that upon return to full consciousness were obeyed. I soon realised that here was a practice which needs to be used with utmost care and discretion.

On one occasion the doctor and I went to a mass-hypnotism demonstration. These public performances have since been severely criticized and rightly discouraged. I am glad, however, that I saw this particular demonstration in the Town Hall of a northern city. Unless one had actually *seen* some of the happenings, the report of them from a third-party would scarcely gain credence.

Everything possible was done to heighten the sense of the hypnotist's power and mystery. To the strains of appropriate "eerie" and compelling music, and after an impressive "build-up" by his assistant, he entered the hall. What he said was amplified through a loud-speaker. He began by inviting those who would like to be cured of smoking to join him on the stage. From various parts of the hall about thirty willing victims trooped on to the platform.

Then he introduced the experiment popularised by Coué, the Frenchman. We were asked to clasp our hands above our heads. When he counted three we were to unclasp them, but he insisted, in smooth hypnotic tones through the amplifier, "you will not be able". He counted, one, two, three. Throughout the hall one heard the sound of people regaining their normal posture, but a few remained with hands joined above their heads. Several on the platform were similarly placed. Those who had resisted his suggestion were weeded out from the rest and sent back to their seats. And members of the audience who were still obeying it, were substituted. Now he had his team of "suggestible" people.

To the delight and astonishment of the audience, he had these people doing some of the oddest and strangest things. Some were sent for an imaginary cycle ride, others shivered from the hypothetical cold, and in another experiment some took off their coats because of purely fictitious heat. One man, the most "suggestible" of all, was hypnotised deeply and made to lie rigid between the seats of two chairs, shoulders on one, feet on the other, whilst the hypnotist and his assistant, weighing together some twenty-seven stones, stood on his body. Having been told that he would remember nothing of what happened, he was restored to consciousness. It was obvious that he had not the slightest recollection of his feat. He was most indignant when the hypnotist told him. Before the night ended, the promise concerning smoking had been fulfilled for many of the initial team. They were given strong suggestions, while hypnotised, that smoking would bring on feelings of nausea. Towards the end of the meeting cigarettes and pipes were produced and lit. It was obvious to the audience that the folk on the platform, at least temporarily, were experiencing the greatest revulsion from a former pleasure.

Between the two stages of this "performance" the doctor and I went back-stage to talk to the hypnotist, who seemed both to be aware of his powers, and of the dangers attaching to these performances. "What I do here," he declared, "is purely for entertainment. We say this in all our announcements."

Before we left the building we saw one young woman in an overwrought state carried through to the room behind the stage. She, in the body of the hall, had been absorbing the hypnotist's instructions, and acting in accordance with them. When we saw her she needed "quietening down" and restoration from the sympathetic hypnotic state.

Today hypnosis is more favourably considered as a medical fact, and demonstrations and discussions have gone forward on radio and television. The phenomenon is acknowledged, even though many scarcely know what to think of it. You will not discover anyone able to tell you exactly how "hypnosis" works nor what it is. All I can say is that I have seen it in operation and have myself "put people to sleep". It is a condition extraordinarily like sleep, and yet different from it. The patient's conscious mind is released from awareness and control. One is in direct touch with the mind's deeper phases.

A case with which we were concerned was of a woman suffering from ex-ophthalmic goitre. Under hypnosis this woman revealed facts concerning her marital life of which she had not given the slightest inkling in previous conversation with the doctor, and this in spite of her great desire to be as helpful and co-operative as possible. Her trouble was an inner fear of the mother-in-law's influence over the man she had married. The fear was so distasteful that she would not recognise it. It was thus a buried fear and it had much to do with her physical condition. By helping her to acknowledge this consciously the doctor led her to a much improved condition, both bodily and mentally.

Again whilst working with this psychiatrist, I shared in a case in which a girl recovered from paralysis. It had certain features reminding one of the Gospel story of the paralytic whom Jesus made to walk. The record in the Gospel tells us of a cure in two stages: the first of them concerned forgiveness. When this was realised, the bodily cure followed as a second stage. Our young friend also needed forgiveness: the human forgiveness of her father.

In this case, and the one previously mentioned, permission has been given to tell what happened. But, even so, this story must be related with reticence. The girl was first brought to the psychiatrist suffering from paralysis of the legs. She could not walk. The doctor, after quietly talking with her, suspected psychological origin of her trouble. Its onset seemed to follow a physical assault suffered a few months before. Uninstructed about sex, the full horror of this event made the girl lose confidence in life, in other people, and consider herself unfit to marry now that "this" had happened.

Part of the story was drawn from her during preliminary talks. During the hypnotic treatment that followed, her bodily condition improved enormously. The neighbours and the people living in her district noticed it. When a paralytic, who cannot move except in a wheel chair, begins to find strength in her legs again and, supported by other people, is able to walk, folk are bound to take note.

Under hypnosis much more was discovered about the assault and the resulting trauma. Then strong suggestions were implanted concerning her renewed ability to walk, and the need to face life with courage and hope. Meanwhile under ordinary waking conditions she was given a right perspective regarding the facts of sex, and told that the possibilities of a husband and a future home were not necessarily denied her.

Over the months this improvement continued until it reached a certain stage. Then, despite whatever was done, there was no further progress.

As a minister brought to share in this case, I felt its wonder and its appeal. What could we do, asked the doctor, to take her a stage further? One day I had an "inspiration". In the home of mother, father and only daughter, the father was the key to the situation! By the nature of the case the girl and her mother would obviously have talked together about what had occurred. Yet in that kind of home it was almost certain that father and daughter had never done so. Wasn't it likely that this girl was feeling that she needed his forgiveness, or at least the assurance of his understanding?

The doctor agreed that this might be the very clue we needed, and a plan of campaign was decided. Under hypnosis the girl was given strong suggestions that next day she should seek an opportunity to ask her father if he had forgiven her for the things that had happened. The father, who was most anxious to help his daughter, was given full information and guidance to ensure maximum co-operation. He was to receive her confession and plea for forgiveness calmly and to talk so lovingly and constructively that it would heal her deep hurt.

All went according to plan. When next we visited the house, the mother was so excited she could hardly tell her story. At midday on the day following our last visit, the family had been at lunch. Towards the end of the meal the mother had left the two alone in the room. Holding on to the chairs and the table the girl had come behind her father and, putting her hands on his shoulder, said, "Dad, I want to know if you've forgiven me for what happened?" He must have played his part wonderfully, for within a few weeks the improvement began for which all had been longing. The barrier had been removed, and within a short time the girl was not only walking without assistance but, what was even more remarkable, was prepared to go unaccompanied into town. Eventually she married and had a child of her own.

I want to revert again to this subject of health and healing, and also to the subject of forgiveness, in later chapters. But here I think it is worth recording what the doctor said after the girl had recovered her health. Both of us had been tremendously impressed by the girl's astonishing recovery. "This case has convinced me," said my medical friend, "that within the human frame there are great forces all too little understood or appreciated even today. The Church and the medical profession ought to co-operate in research into this vast reservoir of inner power."

The influence of mind over body, and body over mind, is increasingly being taken into account in our day and the science of psycho-somatic medicine is advancing rapidly. About this, too, I would like to say more. But now we are not making final deductions about these matters, but using these cases to show the existence of forces within us powerful to aid or hinder. These forces can work great good or great harm. Now we are noticing their existence and their strength.

It is from within-outward that life's current flows. What happens within determines how the exterior life shapes and expresses itself. As we have noticed, this can show in terms of bodily health. The stories in this chapter concern matters which I have personally observed and analysed.

This evidence, of which an immense amount can be assembled, indicates that behind human life are rich reserves of power waiting to be tapped. These forces reveal not only great energy, but also creative potentiality. It is of this that I want to write in the next chapter.

5

Creative Forces

*It is as if a fountain of creative Mind were welling up,
bubbling to expression within prepared spirits. There is
an infinite fountain of lifting power, pressing within us,
luring us by dazzling visions, and we can only say, the
creative God comes within our souls.*

THOMAS KELLY[1]

WHEN considering the power available to the inner
self, the testimony of the artist and the writer needs
attention as well as that of the psychiatrist and physician.

The great artist knows that inspiration comes to him
from *within*. Often he will prefer to say, "from above".
It is indeed from within that inspiration from above
reaches him. He is constantly marvelling at beauty in the
outer world and taking account of its colour, shape and
form. But that is not the source of his best work. Something fuses within him, and the beauty he has seen with
his eyes becomes the raw material through which his inner
self produces creative inspiration.

"My thoughts are not mine," cried Mozart, "they all
come to me—pour into me—from above." Many another
musician has witnessed similarly to the way inspiration has
come *through him*. His conscious mind has not been the
author of his compositions. What has poured into him,
and through him, has come through the doorway of his
inner self.

It is when the control of the conscious mind has in
some measure been relaxed that the rich creativity of the

inner self works most effectively. A close study of certain original thinkers in such diverse realms as music, poetry, mathematics, science and art reveals this. Often when people engaged in creative work have reached the point of despair, certain that they cannot find that for which they are looking, the answer arrives without any struggle at all.

There is a striking example of this in what some would regard as the dry-as-dust pages of Church History. The British Church has a few famous figures in the Middle Ages. One of them is Anselm, Archbishop of Canterbury from 1095–1109. Whilst in Normandy, before crossing to this country, he had puzzled for years over the problem of faith. Others had ventured upon what have been called "proofs" of God's existence. Anselm felt there should be some way of expressing, within the compass of a single argument—not of several disconnected arguments—a reasoned demonstration of this.

He tells how at times what he sought seemed almost within his grasp, and at other times it eluded his mind's reach altogether. Finally in despair he resolved to give up his search. Then one day what he thought was completely beyond his ability came to him in a flash, unbidden. The result was a little book, deservedly famous, incorporating what philosophers call the "ontological proof" of the existence of God.[2] Anselm's own account clearly witnesses (1) to his initial desire and endeavour (2) to his despair of ever achieving it (3) to his renunciation of his task—on the level of his conscious mind, and (4) to the sudden arrival of the answer in complete form.

At times there is something slightly exasperating at the way inspiration arrives unbidden as, for example, the story of the Berlioz symphony that was never written. One night, as the composer lay in bed, there ran through his mind the music of an allegro. It was in 2–4 time, in A minor. All was complete. He rose in order to write it down. But because of other pressing claims, he desisted. If he started on such a work it would demand three or four months he could not spare. Next night he heard the music again clearly. He seemed, even, to see it written down, and sang the theme to himself. But, thinking over the same commitments as the night before, he stayed in bed, and finally went to sleep. Upon waking next day, all recollection of the music had gone. The point I want to make is that not a note of the symphony was written down by Berlioz. The lovely music that was lost to him, and to us, had been worked out by, and come through, his deeper self. But he had done nothing to capture it.

The classic story is that of "the man from Porlock". Waking from a dream Coleridge realised he had a poem, complete, only waiting to be put on paper. He started writing, and what he wrote we now know as the fragment, *Kubla Khan*. A "man from Porlock" was suddenly announced, and when the poet returned from seeing what he wanted, the rest of the poem had fled from his mind.

Nikola Tesla, described in a recent biography as *The Giant of Electricity*, once told reporters that his inventions came to him in the way of mental pictures. It was not his habit to make hurried models from initial ideas, and then attempt to perfect these first efforts. He allowed his inner self to do all this for him, needing only to see everything clearly first in mental vision.

John Masefield has described how he came to write *The Everlasting Mercy*.[3] It was at a time when he had almost given up hope of becoming a writer. Though he had diligently applied himself to this end, the way did not seem to open. One spring day, taking a walk through a wood, he looked at a bank carpeted with primroses. A voice (not his own) sounded within him, "The Spring is beginning," and he felt a new hope surge in his heart.

A month later he went for an evening walk through

another copse, delighting in all the beauty about him. He was in a state of immense inner joy because of what he had seen that morning. He came home uphill through the wood, "feeling that the incredible and the impossible were on each side of me." As he passed through a fence dividing the copse from the common beyond, he said to himself, "Now I will make a poem about a blackguard who becomes converted". Instantly the complete poem presented itself. Even before he reached home he had scribbled down the first fifteen to twenty lines. He went on writing the next sixty or so until he knew that he must go to bed. Within three weeks and three days he had finished the work with which his fame began. The story had come to him, and the poem been put in order, by the creative power within.

The intervening month between Masefield's hearing of the voice and that day was not unimportant in the process. It was an incubating period. Masefield tells us that living amidst rural sights and sounds, he spent the time worrying away at his work, "finding no light upon it, yet sure that the promised light would come." It is most impressive to notice that the complete poem ends with a lyrical passage far more Masefield's own statement than that of Saul Kane. It takes us back to that first spring day when Masefield heard the voice, "The Spring is beginning."

> O lovely lily clean,
> O lily springing green,
> O lily bursting white,
> Dear lily of delight,
> Spring in my heart agen
> That I may flower to men.[4]

I am not, of course, advocating methods of inactivity and laziness as a means of accomplishing imaginative work. That is not the way this mechanism operates. All the folk we have quoted were people putting every kind of conscious effort into their craft, ceaselessly gathering know-ledge and impressions that would help them. But they came to know that—for them at any rate—the fount of creativity issues from a deeper level. Contrasted with the analysing, reasoning, systematizing abilities of the conscious mind, the inner self possesses infinitely greater originative power.

Bertrand Russell, the sceptic philosopher, has confessed to this discovery. If now he has to write on some difficult subject he thinks about it intensely for a few days or hours, and then "gives orders, so to speak, that the work is to proceed underground." Returning to the subject after an interval of a few weeks he finds the difficulties resolved. "Before I discovered this technique," he reports, "I used to spend the intervening months worrying because I was making no progress . . . whereas now I can devote them to other pursuits."[5]

I have found this true in my own experience. The best ideas do not come from reasoning; they emerge, as it were, from a deeper strata of one's being. One learns to be very grateful for these "inspirations".

We can say, then, that the power within is in part a creative force. Much of our mental inspiration is attributable directly to it, rather than to the conscious self. We have noted, in the previous chapter, that this power can reinforce bodily mechanisms, enabling a little undersized man to stretch himself rigid between two chairs, taking on him the weight of two heavily-built men. What needs to be noticed is that, whether hypnotized or not, the ability to do this was there within. This power can also work out destructively both in mind and body, bringing a full-grown girl to a state of paralysis and fear. We have observed, too, that it obeys orders and suggestions. In this chapter we have established its connections with creativity.

There are two considerations emerging directly from this, (1) the material which we "feed into" our deeper mind must be watched most carefully. In the chapter on Seed Influences we noticed the way seed-ideas take root and develop. "You can't make bricks without straw," is a popular saying that reminds us that if our creative powers are to work they must be provided with the best of material. Straw is not as necessary for making bricks as the proverb would suggest, but good clay is. We must beware of receiving into the mind mere chaff, stones and stubble. We must avoid feeding on poor ideas and soiled notions.

(2) Learning to harvest the possibilities from this creative realm we must note, again, the value of silent, reflective periods amidst our busy-ness. In these quiet times there is opportunity for the "bubbling up" from these inner regions of which Marcus Aurelius spoke. For a person engaged in creative work to be ceaselessly busy, and never allow for intervals of quiet and meditation, is comparable to a person granted the privilege of half-an-hour with a genius and then filling the time with a personal monologue.

Our conscious directing self is the controller and organiser of these deeper potentialities. These inner powers can either be squandered and abused or invited to inspired co-operation. It is *our responsibility.*

Some psychologists maintain that we are not to be held responsible for whatever in our conduct comes from hidden sources. They say, "Basic motivations come from within, and therefore we cannot be blamed for them." I maintain, however, that what we "feed into" our minds by thought and environmental influences over the years is in large measure responsible for the nature of our inner selves, and for the impulses and desires proceeding from them. Of course I am not discussing the unbalanced mind, but that of the average person. We are meant to be in control and must recognize that, under God, we are the captains of our soul.

Certainly God holds us responsible. As the next chapter

will remind us, our Lord tells us that in the day of judgment we shall have to give account of "every idle word". What that means we shall go on to investigate: but it clearly does not mean we are allowed to evade our responsibility for the kind of person that the Stranger Within really is.

6

Every Idle Word

Why even I myself I often think know little or nothing
   of my real life,
Only a few hints, a few diffused faint clews and indirections
I seek for my own use to trace out here.

WALT WHITMAN[1]

FURTHER understanding of the inner self and its workings can be gained in a much more mundane fashion
than by experimenting with hypnotism or observing
genius at work. Anyone who takes the trouble to watch
the casual words and actions of the people he meets daily
can easily gather this evidence for himself.

I want to begin, however, by referring to what is still
a strange field to most of us. We know that it is often part
of psychological treatment that the patient, encouraged
to feel as relaxed as possible in mind and body, should be
induced to relate whatever enters his mind, without any
kind of censorship, relieved of any fear of criticism. What
does the psychologist hope to achieve by this? The answer
is that by careful analysis of this flow of talk he hopes to
obtain an insight into motivations working deep within the
patient's nature. The freer the talking, the less controlled
and censored, the more likely it is that hidden impulses
will be disclosed.

In ordinary conversation the conscious self is very much
in command. Only when we watch ourselves do we discover how much "on guard" we are, choosing what we
shall say and discuss. In the "free association" of the
psychologist's couch, this guard is removed. It is intended

that the patient should be as tactless, as indiscreet as possible. The conversation follows no set course. Under skilled guidance it is remarkable what clues emerge disclosing inner concerns and feelings.

Conditions in ordinary life which approximate to this unguarded, uncensored freedom of the psychologist's couch can be equally revealing. Most of us in our daily living—especially English people—are careful and precise, playing our self-chosen part, tight-lipped and cautious. Occasionally, however, the inner self, or the hidden truth, is revealed at an unguarded moment. For this reason the woman who "prattles" is always a dangerous person. With her no secret is safe. In her prattling she is bound to disclose far more than she intends.

The odd way in which we sometimes forget names, or words, and the strange manner in which some of our mistakes occur in speech and writing needs to be looked at carefully.[2] Often we are led into this mechanism of forgetting, not by any trick of the conscious mind, but by our inner self. A name is perhaps associated with some form of anguish or pain, and our memory conveniently becomes inoperative. Similarly verbal slips sometimes indicate the disturbance of our attention through an obtruding thought (called up not by our conscious mind, again, but from the inner self). Behind these lapses of speech is sense and purpose, but it is important to note that the purpose is temporarily hidden from the conscious mind. This vagary of behaviour reveals something of our true inner self. It concerns factors operative there. The Stranger Within is making his presence known.

Here is an example of the way this works. (Maybe you will feel that this, like some of the other illustrations I shall use, is a little far-fetched. But this is exactly how such incidents occur). Two women are talking; one enquires after a third party known to both of them. Without thinking the first woman uses the third party's maiden name. When her attention is drawn to this, she is first surprised and then a little nettled. She has to admit that the real reason for the slip is not that this was the name by which she first knew the woman, but that she herself had once hoped to marry the woman's husband. Thus bitter resentment in her deeper self blocks the memory of the third party's married name. It is the maiden name that rises to her lips.

All of us can watch ourselves making similar slips. They are often an indication of deeper motivations working from within.

Hostesses who have been entertaining an unwelcome guest have been known, at the moment of farewell, to reveal unwittingly their true feelings. A word has been changed and instead of the formal, "I hope you will come to see us again," they have been horrified to hear themselves say, "I hope you won't come to see us again." Perhaps tired after the stress of the occasion, the guard maintained throughout the irritating visit has momentarily been relaxed—and the truth is out!

Have you known this kind of thing to happen when writing an uncongenial letter? We have done our duty, expressing the sentiments expected and then, for a second or two, writing semi-automatically we find we have set down something very different from what we meant. "I hope it will be convenient for you to come," is what we were intending, but when we came to re-read we find, "I hope it will be inconvenient for you to come." Have you never had to alter a word or re-draft a letter because of some such mistake?

A friend of mine confesses to an unhealthy interest in the alterations in letters that come to him. They are far more revealing, he declares, than what has been left alone!

It must not be thought that what is "revealed" in these ways is always and necessarily unpleasant. What is exposed depends on the condition of the inner self, and on the ideas harboured there. It has always been impressive to me that Mistress Quickly in recounting the way that Falstaff died, told us far more about that swashbuckling knight that she knew. "His nose was sharp as a pen," she reported, "and a'babbled of green fields." In that babbling, Falstaff helps us to see something in his nature we should never have suspected—a real love of the countryside as over against his roystering life in the towns and taverns.

Two thousand years ago our Lord drew attention to the importance of the "idle words" men speak. The complete paragraph in which this reference occurs is important, for it demonstrates our Lord's concern about the inner self. "Either make the tree good, and his fruit good; or else make the tree corrupt, and his fruit corrupt: for the tree is known by his fruit . . . out of the abundance of the heart the mouth speaketh. A good man out of the good treasure of the heart bringeth forth good things: and an evil man out of the evil treasure bringeth forth evil things. But I say unto you, That every idle word that men shall speak, they shall give account thereof in the day of judgment. For by thy words thou shalt be justified, and by thy words thou shalt be condemned."

The adjective translated in A.V. as "idle" means "careless", "thoughtless", as many of the recent translations have indicated. It is not that light, flippant words are unworthy of the high seriousness of a follower of Jesus (this is what some commentators have argued!) but that unguarded words reveal the self—and what they reveal may be something very shabby indeed. It is this inner self—the real, not the apparent or "wished" self—which is finally accepted or rejected (condemned or approved) at the Day of Judgment.

"I didn't know I had it in me," we cry. But we had! It was there. The crucial moment, as well as the idle word, will disclose it. What a surprise the denial of his Lord was to Peter. It was no surprise to Jesus, who knew Peter better than he knew himself. "Though all men deny thee, yet will not I." "You will, Peter, and after it has happened, you really will become Rock. When that time comes, pass on some of this needed strength to your brethren."[3] In the moment of testing, in spite of his deep attachment to his Lord, the instincts of a lifetime asserted themselves. Deeply ingrained in Peter was the habit of getting out of a situation by any method that offered. The inner self, that Jesus knew and Peter did not, swiftly took control in this moment of danger.

It is very difficult for some people to come to self knowledge. Our conscious minds are so much in evidence. We have built up a picture of ourselves, concerning which our surface mind does its best to keep us in good heart. Our real motives are often clearer to those who calculatingly observe us. Sometimes unknowingly and sometimes quite deliberately, we cover over what we are doing with "rationalizations" or excuses. Others watch our actions, and draw different conclusions from those we wish to convey.

But our face-saving devices deceive no one. "I'm giving way to younger men," says the footballer or athlete. What has really happened is that he can no longer perform as once he could: but the truth expressed like that is unpleasant. So he says to others—and to himself—"I'm retiring to give place to the footballers of the future."

If we take the trouble to notice some of the ways in which the Stranger Within reveals himself, we shall learn a great deal about ourselves. This is what the expert psychiatrist sets out to do: to introduce us to ourselves. His task is to make us ready to reckon with our real self. When he has done that the major part of his work is done. It is for us to do the rest.

Among the records now available of psycho-analysis as experienced by the patient, is one by a skilled reporter, daughter of a New York attorney, named Lucy Freeman.[4]

Its special value is that it comes from someone who resisted each succeeding stage of self-revelation, and who yet had to acknowledge the truth, benefiting enormously.

Lucy, who in 1941 became a general news reporter for the New York *Times*, had for years suffered from much ill-health. In spite of expensive and varied treatments she secured no relief. At the end of World War II another period of illness, associated with nervous anxieties and irrational fears, drove her to see a specialist.

The psychiatrist to whom she went was in no hurry, and much of her regimen consisted in free association as outlined at the beginning of this chapter. Soon, however, her bodily condition showed a great improvement. Her buried fears were uncovered and she began to realise, and to deal with, some of the hidden emotions carried over from childhood. "What do you discover about yourself?" was a question she was continually asked. Lucy's story is of a battle for self-knowledge, and of peace at the end when she was willing to accept her inner self, and build up on the basis of this new knowledge.

One of the things evident even at this distance of time concerning Jesus of Nazareth is that He was able to pierce through the outer to the inward man. As John said about Him, "He knew what was in man." When He met with Zaccheus, and the woman by the well, He saw the true person hidden from their neighbours.

This faculty possessed by our Lord in such fulness is found in a lesser degree in numbers of others. A discerning few can reach through to the inner self. We have our "hunches" as we say.

People know "you" better than the mask you may be wearing. "Why do they misread my motives?" we ask: the fact is that, all too often, they have got through to motivations we have hidden from ourselves.

O. Henry in one of his stories describes an artist whose work was so wonderful that nobody would engage him:

"his brush revealed qualities which his sitters had always taken great pains to hide: his portraits were a kind of mental X-ray."

The fact that we have this ability to pierce the mask, and to recognize one another's inner personality helps us to understand how it is we shall know one another in the after-life. As Paul tells us in 1 Corinthians 15, we shall no longer possess this body, but a "spiritual body". Yet, we shall immediately be known. Dives and Lazarus in our Lord's parable, when translated into the after-life's new dimension *apart from the old body,* immediately recognized each other. This is because what passes beyond death is the *real* self.

All through our life we may be unaware of the Stranger. But be sure other people are not ignorant. They realise that we are not like the mask we turn to them, by which we actually deceive ourselves. To others, the Stranger Within has been continually declaring himself. We know now that he has been doing this in some measure by little tricks of behaviour, in our idle words, and chance actions.

One of the disconcerting things about the idea of death and the judgment is that the mask is finally removed and our real self revealed. By this, says our Lord, we shall be approved or condemned.

7

A Place of Communion

Strength calmed by strength, moving inwards to God.
M. LOUISE HASKINS[1]

THE inner self is in reality a vast meeting place. For each of us it is the focal point of our world. Though outside exist the oceans of space, and though our lives are puny and unimportant, it is from this centre outwards that we, as experiencing beings, come to our knowledge of all that is.

Here then we meet the within and the without. Here all the impressions from sight, hearing, taste, touch and smell, are collected and interpreted and make contact with the creative powers operating from inner sources. Here mind and body interact. Here, in some measure, past, present and future come together, for through our inner selves we have access at the one time to past memories, present experiences and hopes and fears about the future. Here, too, time and eternity confront one another: for the inner self is the point of correlation between the data of this present world, governed and guided by time, and the eternal timeless world.

> *I am the owner of the sphere,*
> *Of the seven stars and the solar year,*
> *Of Caesar's hand and Plato's brain,*
> *Of Lord Christ's heart and Shakespeare's strain.*

If these words of Emerson's are in any sense true, it is because in us is this meeting place. Within our inner self can be gathered something of the ideas of all the ages. Through reading and contacts with others we accumulate and assimilate knowledge.

Still further, the inner self is the meeting place between the powers in us that are almost entirely unconscious and those rising into consciousness. It is also the arena where good and evil struggle for ascendancy. Here, too, we experience joy and happiness: from the orchestration resulting here rises the great feeling-tone of our lives—the ground-bass behind the music played by our surface selves.

Not only are we dealing at this focal point with ideas and sense impressions, but also the full effect of other people's influence, and come to know the deepest interchange of life on the level of spirit with spirit.

What emerges as the expression of one man's inner self has power, for good or ill, to quicken other lives. And as other men meet these influences they have power to reinterpret and alter them. In this present century the process has been observable in the philosophy coming from Karl Marx.

It might be said that *Das Kapital* bears upon it the stamp of an inner life full of conflict. From the embroilment of his inner struggle, Marx looked out on the world and saw it as a place of strife: the "haves" and the "have-nots" locked in a war bound to end, eventually, he thought, with the victory of the proletariat, and the establishment of the classless society.

Marx was not consciously working with evil intent when he wrote his book, the most explosive since the Bible. Burning within him, and forming part of the cauldron of his emotions, was a passionate concern for justice. This blazed in this anti-religious Jew as fiercely as within his compatriot Amos centuries before, brooding on the wrongs suffered by the poor and needy. "Each for all and all for each" is not a motto applied cynically to a millennium so far removed that no one needs to bother about it, nor a slogan invented as bait to draw idealists into the struggle. It is a cry rising from the inner self of a man desiring, as ardently as any Amos, that "justice roll down like waters and righteousness like a mighty stream."

Unfortunately Marx linked his inner passion with a false philosophy of class struggle. In connection with the latter the doctrine was preached that anything was permissible which would hasten the revolution. The ideal days of the classless millennium could, apparently, be brought nearer by any kind of method, however unjust and intolerable! Doubly was this permissible since, by Marx's reasoning, the forces of history decree this final phase as inevitable. By lies, treachery, fifth column activity, and war, one is but shortening the intervening years of misery and waiting.

The twists in Marx's philosophy and the projection of his own inner struggle presented a golden opportunity to those looking for a revolutionary textbook. Lenin and his associates both fed on and applied its doctrine. Emerging thus from the realm of this poisonous theory, Moscow Communism is confirmed in all that is disruptive, becoming the instrument of power blocks with their new form of imperialism. As the steamroller system smashes on its remorseless way, man as an individual does not count. The demonic figure of the totalitarian state—with its omnicompetence guaranteed by communist theory—overrides all individual considerations.

Thus Communism, born in reaction against injustice, has by the evil intentions of its leaders (working from within their natures) been turned from what was good and splendid into a world menace.

So many movements for emancipation and nationalization in the modern world exhibit similar features and are subject to the same fatal flaws. What is idealistic in these movements is twisted because those meant to express it are personally overcome by greed and lust for power. The motives which befoul the stream of human yearning after better things have their origin deep within human nature.

The Stranger Within has thus enormous influence over men in the mass. Behind the outbreaks of mob violence and the cataclysm of war are inimical feelings working within the inner life of millions. If we are to deal effectively with the forces disrupting our society, then, as individuals, as churches and as nations, we must learn to go far deeper than we have been doing to effect a lasting cure.

*   *   *   *

In Part 1 of this book we have been concerned to establish the identity and whereabouts of the Stranger Within, and to point to his supreme importance. The inner self, the guiding factor behind our lives, has been too little recognized and indeed, often totally ignored. Our inner life must be renewed and safeguarded. We need this for our own sake as individuals, and we need it, together, for the sake of the whole human race. Modern psychiatric science has established beyond doubt the existence of forces hidden within us. We as Christians need to recognize and use them in our daily living.

As Part II will indicate, there is a power able to deal radically with our inner ills and to reinforce all that is creative and splendid within. The same energy can bring us to inner harmony, so that "all our soul and body's powers" follow one central aim and purpose. The power is to be felt in the inner self, the place of meeting: and it is not impersonal but personal.

> There is no need to search so wide,
> Open the door and stand aside—
> Let God in![2]

The greatest fact about the inner self is that it can become a place of encounter and communion with Jesus Christ. Cries Masefield's converted rapscallion, Saul Kane,

O glory of the lighted mind!
How dead I'd been, how dumb, how blind!

Kane had been reached in this place of meeting, as the story evidences and his words reveal.

Thus all of us have found it to be, when we have encountered Christ within our nature. Here, in the power of all that He is, is a force to deal with our disordered inner selves, to bring us unity, and to make our lives of value in the world, to the glory of God the Father.

Recently a man told me how twenty-five years ago his own life had been revolutionized. Three things strongly impressed me. The experience was associated with what psychologists describe as a "photism"—the phenomenon of being surrounded in light. "It was as if there were light within and around me". Then, "It was bound up with Jesus. I felt vividly in touch with Him, and what was happening was all because of Him. I felt clean, whole, made new." For a day or two he lived a life filled with an inexpressible quality, "as if lifted out of this world altogether". Then though he knew that his feet were firmly on the ground again, yet the sense of integration, of a purpose discovered and made real in Jesus, stayed with him, and has developed over the years.

"Light"—all about him; a vivid sense of Jesus, and the knowledge of His presence; leading to integration and the one-pointing of his life.

I elicited some further facts about this light. It was intense. Pressed about its colour he said it hadn't any—perhaps you could say it had a white, misty radiance: it was blazing *light*. It was, he said, like communion within light—all in light around.

You remember how in the account of what happened at Pentecost the writer uses the words, "as of", and "like as": "a sound from heaven as of a rushing mighty wind", "tongues like as of fire". Anyone trying to convey the impressions of authentic spiritual experience is bound to fall back on this kind of language. One is trying to describe the indescribable. It was "like this".

The light that my friend saw was not external at all. It was the reflection throughout his personality of something *within*. There, where this personal encounter was taking place, where Jesus was making Himself known, is the realm where we must look for its origin.

Others of us would have to use language of a different kind to describe our climactic first encounter with our Lord in living power. I would have to say that "it was as if barriers went down: some kind of inner restraint vanished: life was deepened and renewed". Where did this happen? Not in the outside world, but within.

Yet what happens there changes the external world as we are experiencing it. Never had it looked so bright nor the trees so beautiful as that Spring after Christ burst into my inner world.

> *The station brook* to my new eyes
> *Was babbling out of Paradise.*[3]

The story of Paul's conversion is of a similar pattern. The light that blinded him, and the voice he heard, sounded within his own nature: *that* was where they were experienced, far more than in the external world.[4]

I have known many people who have passed through an authentic conversion experience of a far less dramatic order. Some have come very quietly to it, scarcely realising that over a period of deep thinking and praying the change has taken place. Others can point to a definite occasion when all their previous experience clarified. Listening to a preacher, reading the Word of God, walking on the hills, standing by the sea, God revealed Himself to them in power and love. But the basis of what happened is the same. He who has revealed Himself has been received within—the place of communion.

God does not normally come crashing into our nature. He is the seeking God: not the intruder. The picture covered by the words, "Behold I stand at the door and knock" is authentic. This is the realm of encounter, and then of commitment and communion. Whether it is to be all these depends on us.

> *Within, within oh turn*
> *Thy spirit's eyes and learn*
> *...Thy dearest Friend dwells deep within thy soul*
> *And asks Thyself of Thee.*[5]

These are the possibilities providing hope for the human race and its future. When the peoples of the world know this inner contact with God, the fulfilment of our daily prayer will be in sight, "Thy kingdom come, Thy will be done, on earth, as it is in heaven." Instead of the working out of the spirit of malignity, as from satanic Moscow Communism, we shall witness the results of love operating universally. This is the vision worth working for, and praying for—when God shall rule the world through changed individuals in tune with Him, and in harmony with one another.

Part II

Fulfilment

You shall know the truth, and
the truth shall make you free.
                    JESUS.

8

The Way Forward

> *Thou callest me to seek Thy face;*
> *'Tis all I wish to seek;*
> *To attend the whispers of Thy grace,*
> *And hear Thee inly speak.*
>
> CHARLES WESLEY[1]

FOR anyone to deny that God can be met within the self is to ignore the considerable evidence. Countless people, from New Testament times to our own, have witnessed to God's dramatic intervention. In mid-stream their lives have been re-directed. Overnight they have been swung from crime, self-seeking, or indulgence, to something as different as white from black, or day from night. These cases afford striking evidence of change. They have often been so remarkable as to be almost unbelievable to those who previously knew the people concerned. And the change has happened not externally, but within. The results appear in the outward world but the origins lie deep and unseen.

Often this turning round has occurred with the minimum of preparation. Until this happened these folk had little serious idea of Christianity. In understanding they could be described as babes, but in experience they have suddenly leapt forward as giants.

I have known and talked with such people, and I am not in the slightest doubt concerning what has happened to them. Their radiant faces and transformed bearing carry a testimony that needs no words: but they will add, with great humility, and equal firmness, such explanations as: "God has invaded my life," or "He has spoken to me,"

"His light flooded my soul," or "Jesus has shown me a forgiveness that's swallowed my past."

The Cornish poet, Jack Clemo, in his book *The Invading Gospel*, looks back on his own story and says, "It has invaded me completely. . . . Every facet of my natural self—the pagan mystic, the brooding hermit, the baffled individualist—is gone without trace. I have been filled with the joy of the maturing convert who has given his natural fate the slip by surrendering all its possibilities to the Divine Invader."[2]

Such dramatic experiences are, however, exceptional. The sudden revelation, the mystical explosion within, the light bathing one's entire being—these are not usual of day-to-day experiences. For most of us the change from external to vital religion takes place more gradually. Our contact with God has not been of this explosive nature. Our communion has developed along the ordinary channels of regular worship, and daily prayer and meditation.

What is important to recognize is that for us all—the dramatic exceptions and the humble seekers of the more prosaic road—these personal encounters are made through the Stranger Within. It is here that men come face to face with God, and the revelations from the divine occur.

In beginning Part II I want to do so on the level of ordinary experience. We need to know what the *average* Christian can expect in the way of direct revelation, of the knowledge of God, and inner guidance concerning His will.

Is it possible that God will visit *us*? Can *we* establish communion with Him in this place of meeting within the self, and overhear what He is saying to us there? Is guidance possible concerning the conduct and control of *our* lives? Can we, for instance, learn what effective contribution we can make toward world sanity, and the upbuilding of peace and justice? Is it possible, amidst the welter of events, to find what is His intention for us and others?

I believe that there are quite definite answers to all these questions. Throughout the second part of this book we shall be looking at what they involve. Here, in the opening chapter, I want to concentrate more particularly on this question of inner guidance and the establishment of life's true direction. As we set out on the way forward our first consideration must be to discover what God wants us to do with our lives. It is no use discussing techniques and looking for methods of co-operating with the forces of the Stranger Within, unless we are prepared to follow the path God has for us.

It must then first be said that the answers we seek to these deeply personal questions do not always arrive neatly addressed and immediately decipherable. Sometimes we spend much of our lives trying to unravel the secret of our instructions. Often they are like sealed orders which we understand only in battle. But the point is that these orders are obtainable. They come direct from God through the inner self where His voice can be heard, and a sense of His presence known.

All of us need training in these matters—the kind of training we can only give ourselves through patient willingness to listen and obey. To many what God is saying seems to come as a whisper rather than a trumpet blast. That is why the phrase concerning the "still small voice" holds such magic. It is part of our job, however, to learn to distinguish this whisper from all other voices within our nature. Mrs. E. Herman, in one of her books, pictures a radio officer on his first trial at sea, putting his previous training to the test. The faint scratches, the distant oscillations mean now more than ever they did. By means of his dedicated listening he has come to recognize the voice that is calling *him*. He can single it out from all others, tuning into it so that its message comes loud and clear.

"My sheep hear my voice," said our Lord Jesus. He said this with absolute confidence. If we are His we should be able to know whenever His voice sounds within. It is different from that raised by our own subconscious desires and imaginings.

Many years ago I had an unforgettable experience of inner guiding. It had to do with a relationship which was proving increasingly dangerous. My inner mentor announced quite definitely that this friendship must cease for both our sakes. Though I was already beginning to recognize whose voice this was, the decision seemed harsh and cruel. All my surface inclinations were against it. I tried to argue the case in my prayers, but this inner conviction would not yield. In the end I recognized it as right. Most painfully, and feeling something of a brute, I made the break. The most testing time, however, was to come when the attempt was made to renew the friendship. Looking back it seems to me as if I were brought through that experience with Someone helping me from within, reinforcing my will, which at the time was very shaky indeed. It was one of the most perilous stretches of the road I have so far travelled. I *know* that I received help and direction. And it reached me *from within*.

When first venturing on the Christian way an older man gave me some advice for which I've never ceased to be grateful. It concerned the sentence, "Thy word is a lamp unto my feet, and a light unto my path." "That," said the veteran, "is exactly how I've found it: always light for the next step. The old-fashioned lantern did not give you light for the far distances, but you *could* see where you were putting your feet. You can always discover the next step God wants you to take. Take it. You've light enough. And after that, there'll be enough for the next... And so on." The experienced campaigner was right. So it has been for me: enough light for the next step ahead —together with a clear indication of one's general direction from the start: all this God gives. I know it now for myself.

In this intimate contact with God in the inner place of

communion life becomes increasingly Christ-centred, and because of this life's direction becomes clear. Everything is accepted in the light of His judgment. Under His command one ventures out to love, and to serve.

The time may come when we begin to realise the need in the world around us and feel, under God, the stirring of powers that in some measure can answer it. Then we receive a "call". The need is there. The answer is found as a result of the true self, the Stranger Within, acting in affinity with God and with His Will. Here is the opportunity for the disciple to show in life and service such excellence as shall be something of a portrayal of his Lord.

The outworking of all we have been considering is, thus, important beyond measure. The goal we set ourselves is an integrated personality living usefully in God's world and fulfilling His purposes. The way towards this goal is made possible by the continual communion with God which we call prayer.

The simple faith of a woman I knew many years ago guided her along this path of duty. She lacked any advantages or education or ability, and would have been the first to say that she was a very ordinary person. She took in hand a Sunday-school class of which, for a brief time, I was a very unruly member. At that stage, quite candidly, I thought her class provided us with a good opportunity for a rag-about. What patience Miss Lamble showed!

Much later she moved to another part of the country; but she kept in touch. There came a time when a young man who had been a member was sent to prison for a serious crime. Miss Lamble wrote to one of us, "So-and-so is to be in prison for eighteen months. When he comes out, will you meet him and stand by him, and see him through?" At the end of the period she wrote again. From the distance that separated her from those who once had been her "boys", and in spite of the passing of time that might have separated her still more, she was exercising her deep sense of duty and concern. We knew that she followed us with her prayers. What has been the influence of those prayers no one can tell.

Many have come to see that this spirit of "caring" is one of Christianity's hallmarks. It is, however, not something artificially to be induced by attention to the mere mechanics of showing interest in others. That way lies pretence, and the kind of play-acting which Jesus condemned. Our compassion needs to have deeper springs than that. We begin by listening within to the voice of our Master. He will lead us along these paths, and change our inner motivation, if we will let Him.

One of the classic stories of this change and of the acceptance of inner guidance is that of St. Francis. Three times the voice sounded within his soul. It was the same voice and the same guidance. Since it came from within, and was touched off by circumstances from without, it had to suffer misinterpretation by the surface mind, and by dominant inclinations. First Francis Bernadone thought he was meant to be a young soldier. Popular young man that he was, he put himself at the head of a troop marching from Assisi in one of the petty wars of the period. From that venture he returned, after a year's imprisonment, ill and disillusioned. This was not the path, and he knew it.

"Build my church, Francis," the voice seemed to be saying. He heard it as he sat amidst the ruins of St. Damian's. And Francis went about this literally, restoring the ruined walls, doing the work by hand, and selling bales of his father's cloth in order to buy the stones. This was not the way either, nor the method. He was not to build the church by what was virtually stealing. What was this guidance within him, struggling to be born? Finally Francis came to know what it was: it was to be an ordinary, humble, faithful follower of his Lord, prepared to do the meanest task for Him. So he would become a soldier—in the army of peace. And so he would build Christ's church, not externally with stones and mortar, but within, in the hearts of men.

Is all this relevant today? Again and again I have been impressed with the way modern young men and women have come to discover God's will for them in the path of vocation and service. The conviction has come from within, sometimes going completely against all surface inclinations, training, and the wishes of loved ones. Now they know, and if you ask them how they know they will say, "God has told me. I have heard His voice within," or they will say, "I have an inner conviction about this that nothing can shake." The conditions have arrived by which someone has put himself, or herself, into the way of recognizing God's intention for their personal living—how they fit into His plan.

Two things are necessary in order to find the way forward. First we must have a passionate desire to discover God's will. And then we must offer Him a personality as completely integrated as we can make it, prepared to answer "Yes" to whatever He asks.

No one has ever acted with greater force, or decision, than Jesus. It is worth examining some of His statements in John's Gospel relative to this. They could not be more emphatically expressed. He says that His words, His deeds, His judgments are not His—they are the Father's.[3] "As I hear, I judge." He and the Father "are one". In His case, what He did, and said, and was, came from a self completely integrated with the Father, knowing continually the guidance coming from within.

Do you remember the words of an impressionable young man, who stood in the Temple at Jerusalem in the years that a great king died? There he saw a vision. The Greater than all earthly kings was revealing Himself. Within his own mind he heard the echo of a voice saying, "Whom shall I send, and who will go for us?" The youth made the only fitting answer to this kind of call when it sounds within our inner nature, "Here am I: send me."

When we know that the voice is God's it demands obedience, and, remember, whatever He asks of us He makes possible. What is needed is to keep close to Him. Now, especially, we need the regular, daily habit of prayer and communion. Thus we are enabled to maintain our service, work out our sense of commission, and clarify our "call".

As we turn to consider consistent, daily prayer we discover that the key to this, too, is found not in outward forms and procedures. Our true praying is done in the realm within.

9

Steps in Prayer

We may pray most when we say least,
and pray least when we say most.

St. Augustine[1]

IF need be the aeroplane pilot of today is able to fly "blind". He is guided by a radio beam, to which the instruments on his panel are attuned. With increasing sensitivity the Christian similarly comes to know when he is on the true path or off it.

These indications come through his inner nature. It is there that God "inly speaks" and reveals His will. It is there, too, that prayer springs to life, and the channel of vital communication is established. It is true that we formulate our prayers with our surface mind, but the centre of our real praying is located within. We may voice our prayers aloud and look upwards as we pray, but this is symbolic, no more. The lines of communication do not run that way. The path of true praying proceeds from the within to the Innermost.

A great Christian leader whom I knew told me of an astonishingly frank conversation he had with a very worldly-minded woman. "God hasn't answered my prayers for my boy, Robert," she complained. "Hasn't he?" replied my friend, "I thought He'd answered them rather well." "How can you speak like that? You know that for years I've prayed that he'd become a keen Christian and enter the life of the Church. Instead, he's climbing to the top of his profession and doesn't seem interested in religion

77

at all." "Tell me honestly, my dear, haven't you worked and schemed, and moved heaven and earth for his advancement? Hasn't your first concern been that Robert should be a great 'success'?" "Yes, I've always wanted him to get on. . . . But what about my prayers?"

"What about them indeed?" echoed the other. "What you framed with your mind weren't your prayers. I'll tell you what was: this fierce ambition you've always had for your boy. And if you're honest you'll have to admit that that prayer is being satisfactorily answered just now."

Prayer, as James Montgomery says, is "the soul's sincere desire"—and the sincere desire is the one that rises not from our lips, but from the Stranger Within. The gateway to all that prayer is, and all it involves, is in the inner self. What we *are* there, and what we *desire* there constitute our real praying, no matter what we articulate with our lips or formulate with our surface minds. It is also through the inner self that so much of the answer to our praying, so far as it concerns ourselves, begins to flow.

Notice how, in true communion with God, our conflicting desires can be resolved. Not always does our destiny coincide with the path of our choice. When, because of the abdication of his brother, kingship was thrust upon the late George VI it was most unwelcome. Reading between the lines of his official biography we can appreciate how at the time his strong sense of duty was reinforced by a deep personal religion.

The story is told that on the night before the Coronation, the Dean of Westminster received a telephone call from the King. "I want to come to the Abbey tonight," he announced. "Certainly, sir. I will be there to receive you." "No, don't do that," the King replied. "I want you to see that the postern door is left open. I wish to come into the Abbey and I wish to be alone." So that night the King kept a vigil of prayer at the altar where on the morrow the pomp and circumstance of the coronation would take place. It was the best of all preparations for what awaited him. In the quiet, alone, the King found reassuring and stabilising contact with God.

Prayer is not something, however, to which we fly just on special occasions, or when under intense pressure. King and commoner alike must discover how to make it a regular part of daily life. There is a *discipline of prayer*. And for this regular praying, too, we must find a place of quiet. We need this in order that we should find the inner door at which to knock, and in order to foster this inward speaking and inward listening.

About this we must be definite. *You* will know the place and the time of day when you can best achieve this. Some years ago, when busily occupied in the city, I used to go to one of the city churches during the lunch hour. For the time available, ten or fifteen minutes, I could always find peace there. Our Lord often chose the hillside before dawn.

Having settled these problems of location, the next suggestion about prayer is a very obvious one: it is *to begin*. Probably that means, for most readers, to begin again. You may not know it, but the way so many of the great figures of the past won through was by sheer persistence. Most of us need a dogged determination in connection with prayer. This way of communion that looks so easy proves to be most difficult. We find dissuasions at every point. Brother Lawrence did not come to his Practice of the Presence in five minutes, nor even in five years, but after a lifetime of starts and re-starts. "The perseverance of the saints," said Alexander Whyte of Edinburgh, "consists in ever new beginnings."

Begin then. And happy are you if in that beginning you experience the glad assurance of God's Love and Mercy surrounding you, and the joy of acceptance as a child of God. All these I experienced when as a young Christian, after a lapse of years, I re-started praying.

The next suggestion I would pass on is to find some help in your methods.[2] Remember that what is one person's best way is not necessarily right for somebody else. Find your own way, and take leave to experiment and change your procedure from time to time. As long ago as 1934 Dr. Leslie Weatherhead prepared a card set out in columns for every day of the week. In these columns were differing suggestions for each day covering the elements of Adoration, Thanksgiving, Confession, Petition, Intercession, Dedication, and Meditation. It was called *Ten Minutes a Day*. Beginners, and even those more advanced, might be well advised to use such a card. It will guide them into most useful devotional habits.[3]

One of the best preparations for prayer comes from associating it with Bible reading. I have found it useful to follow the definite scheme of a Bible Reading association. In my morning quiet time, after remembering into whose presence I seek to enter, and recollecting that my worship of Him must be from within, "in spirit and in truth", I read the Bible passage suggested for the day. I do this before consulting the "Notes" on the reading. Then I have found it useful to jot down the ideas that come while meditating on the passage. Only after this do I look at the "Notes" and check my own impressions with those of the writer. The climax of this meditation is quite naturally the act of prayer. And I know I have made a mistake if I rush too swiftly from active prayer without giving time for listening. Prayer is a two-way traffic. It is learning to find God, and being found by Him, as Tennyson says,

> *Speak to Him, thou, for He hears,*
> *and Spirit with Spirit can meet—*
> *Closer is He than breathing,*
> *and nearer than hands and feet.*

We have been speaking of the discipline of prayer. It is also useful to think of it as an attitude to be cultivated, a constant state of mind in which we live and do everything: "the Christian's native breath".

Scripture encourages us to something which, at first sight, seems utterly impracticable. Paul says, "Pray without ceasing". How can this possibly be done in the workaday world we know: and even if it could, wouldn't it involve an unnatural, strained, artificial way of living? What is being suggested, however, is the cultivation of a constant inner motivation: what Brother Lawrence meant by the Practice of the Presence of God. This is something attempted not in the outer world but within. It is mental praying, and can be continued—once we learn the secret— when our conscious mind is busy with other things. So far from making life "unnatural" it is the way to a life continually renewed, joyous and powerful.

At the start, we will need to invoke the conscious mind's fullest co-operation. And at no point shall we need more exhortation to keep determinedly at this. Remember: "The perseverence of the saints consists in ever-new beginnings."

The secret of what we are seeking to do is to confirm ourselves in a continual state of resting in God. We can emphasise this relationship, and help to make it inwardly real, by saying (aloud if need be and if we are alone) "I am Thine"; or we can just use the word "Thine", repeating this silently and inwardly throughout the day, remembering and resting in the wonder of this relationship with our heavenly Father.

At another time we can make our initial mental prayer a realisation of deep thanksgiving. Thinking of all we owe, we murmur to God an infinite, "Thanks". Throughout the day that is the keyword for our mental praying. Or, as we go about the world, the very name of "Jesus" may be our shield and watchword. To spend a day praying His name in this way of ceaseless, interior prayer is an experience indeed.

One further thing needs to be said, for what I am advocating is not the "vain repetitions" which our Lord attacked. In the realms of magic and superstition, to invoke the name of a god is to bring him on the scene in power. So the heathen believes there is efficacy in incantations involving a string of names. In uttering them he hopes he may pronounce the right one and invoke the god powerful in that situation. Our form of "ceaseless prayer" is far removed from this pagan practice. It involves something not meaningless but very full of meaning, not done from motives of superstition, but encouraging a continual resting upon God: a furthering of the relationship already existing between us. "Ceaseless praying" enables this to be built into our lives.

These are some of the ways to discovery. Enough has been said to invite us into these immense regions where we can speak to God and where, too, we can hear Him "inly speak".

A few years ago, in his *Efficiency Magazine*, which circulates among business people, H. N. Casson wrote an Editorial concerning a man born a negro slave who became famous. "If I were asked," Casson wrote, "what living man had the worst start and the best finish, I would say Dr. Carver. It is a great loss to us that we have no one like him in England."

George Washington Carver was a great man in more ways than one. He became one of the world's foremost biological chemists. His scientific discoveries, and his application of them in developing new industries and new possibilities for his own negro people living in America's deep south, show his mind to have been one of the most creative of our time.

The man himself discovered the secret of any success that came to him in his relationship with God. Listen to him discussing his praying, "My prayers seem to be more of an attitude than anything else. I indulge in very little lip service, but ask the Creator silently, daily, and often many times a day, to permit me to speak to Him through the three great kingdoms of the world which He has created—the animal, mineral, and vegetable kingdoms, to understand their relations to each other, and our relations to the Great God Who made all of us. I ask Him daily and often momently to give me wisdom, understanding, and bodily strength to do His will; hence I am asking and receiving all the time."[4]

Would you like to live in this intimate communion, asking and receiving all the time? You can, by beginning this conversation now—in the depths of your being. You can speak to God there. The place of communion is within.

And for all this to become vital, there is a determining attitude, a set of the inner self, that must be discovered. We need the spirit of faith, about which we shall be thinking in the next chapter.

10

By Faith We Live

Man cannot live without faith.

ERICH FROMM[1]

BEFORE we can pray with power, we need faith. Without this we are working in a vacuum. Our prayers are mere words, our desires and thoughts rebound upon ourselves without reaching God.

"All things," said Jesus, "whatsoever ye shall ask in prayer, believing"—which here means "having faith"—"ye shall receive." It is not sufficient to know that there is, as it were, a switch connecting us with divine potential, nor to discover that this operates in the realm within. We need to switch it on in order to make the current flow.

Faith links us inwardly with the eternal and spiritual. It enables our conscious self to perceive the spiritual reality that is there, and then to hold on to it and live by it in confidence and trust. It is thus a first principle of what Goethe calls the inner universe, and of the highest importance. It has been described as the hand which grasps what God offers. The grasping is done within and connects us with a vast unseen universe outside. And it is part of a total attitude by which we are prepared now to become involved to the roots of our being, moving forward to do things, accepting the divine adjustment, obeying God's commands, and venturing in terms of living.

In spite of this—or perhaps because of this—faith is often a mystifying conception. Particularly do younger people find it difficult to grasp. We who are older have, perhaps, come to recognize it for what it is only after long struggle. So often we think and speak of it axiomatically. But the teenagers amongst us are often baffled. What does it really mean? they ask. They are urged to use it before they have been through life's hard battle. Teenagers have not yet been *forced* to the discovery as some of us have. They must therefore be encouraged to have faith in faith!

Modern youngsters have an added difficulty in that they are reared in an atmosphere of scientific materialism. The very notion of faith seems to some of them an irrational survival from past ages. Science deals with facts, faith with myths and fancies. In our modern world we are supposed to use reason and search for truth. In the past men "believed" what they were told, and had "faith" in what the Church declared as revealed truth—that is how many of them think. The tragedy is that by this misunderstanding of faith multitudes are kept from venturing through the inner door. They fail to discover the Stranger Within; and they never try the way of prayer because the initial faith by which prayer rises to God is missing.

What a difference it would make if they would realise, as Erich Fromm points out, that we cannot live without faith. Like Moliere's *Bourgeois Gentilhomme*, who all his life had been speaking prose without knowing it, we can discover that we have been continually employing this faculty. Let us look at some of the ways in which we all use it.

Faith ordinarily is an everyday attitude of confidence and trust. By means of it we make our ventures. We do not have to test everything before using it, nor stop to ask its meaning, nor examine its credentials.

For example, we have no option but to trust the forces of nature, sowing our seeds in the earth, confident of a harvest. We go forward into the future certain the rains will fall and the sun shine. Every time we sleep we indulge in a gigantic gesture of trust, resigning ourselves to unconsciousness in the certainty of waking in the morning. Every time we ride in a public vehicle, or travel by air, we rely on the safety of the apparatus and the skill of those in charge. We put our money into the bank, and expect the cheques we draw to be honoured (always granting we have sufficient funds!). Habitually we accept statements from reliable sources which we have no reason to doubt. Many of us have never been, nor are likely to go, to India or China. Yet we accept the fact of their existence, and take all kinds of action based on such hypotheses.

Then there is the aspect of faith which can be likened to a daring leap into the unknown. We do not take this irrationally—we take it to test hypotheses we have come to accept. It is because we have come to believe in them that we decide to prove them. This is a use of faith to be observed every day in the secular world. The research worker and the inventor cannot live without this continual challenge.

The scientific innovator is repeatedly being brought to the point where he has to take this leap. He needs to do this in order to evolve any new hypothesis. In eager anticipation, he forges ahead of previous knowledge and then, by testing, verifies the truth (or falsehood) of his idea. By this process the new fact—entered into by faith—becomes part of accepted knowledge.

Edison, the great inventor, once remarked to a friend, "As I analyse my reactions to thoughts and ideas which appear in my mind, I feel that the mere fact that I have an idea is proof that the same source which gave me the idea will also show me how to work it out, provided I hold on." Jules Verne, many of whose predictions have been fulfilled, said, "One man will be able to do what another imagined." The project of space travel so recently accomplished, is itself a venture of faith on the part of the

86

astronaut, as well as of those whose researches and plans lay behind the achievement.

There is another aspect of faith affecting personal relationships. The child has implicit faith in its parents. Young people coming to maturity are willing to entrust themselves and their future in marriage to someone whom they have known scarcely a month or two. So much of this trust concerns intangible factors and unseen forces. But we do not hold back from personal contacts because of these unknowns, nor do we require a guarantee. In our deepest ties we depend entirely on the faith we have in one another.

So faith is a faculty used in varying degree by all throughout the world. Great numbers of those who employ it would not necessarily give it its right name, but Erich Fromm is right: without faith it is literally impossible to live.

Faith enters into its fulness, however, in the religious sphere. For this is the faculty by which contact is established with the spiritual world and we learn its living power. By means of this we can know, and accept, God's forgiveness. By means of it we receive all He offers, identifying ourselves with what we see in Christ, and in His Cross and Resurrection. By means of it great Gospel facts become not happenings of long ago but manifestations of eternal truth and eternal law which we accept *now*. It is also by faith that we make a personal commitment of ourselves to God and enter into relationship with Him. By it we know and trust Him.

This vital link with the spiritual dimension can be made only through the inner self. The man who, in the presence of Jesus, cried, "Lord, I believe (I have some faith), help thou my unbelief" (lack of faith), was voicing just this. In the Master's presence he found himself able to accept the possibility of his son's cure, and to say "Yes" to the incredible hope that God was bringing him in Jesus. Yet he knew that within him there were still barriers—doubts and fears—which had to be broken down. Realising this he appealed for aid. "You help me in those depths where I cannot reach. Help me there where I feel not faith, but the complete lack of it." What a discerning cry that was! How that man speaks for us all.

We can also understand the longing the disciples felt in His company. "Lord," they cried, "increase our faith." The reply is revealing. At first sight it seems almost irrelevant. "If you had faith as a grain of mustard seed, you might say unto this sycamine tree, Be thou plucked up by the roots, and be thou planted in the sea; and it should obey you." Ignoring the obvious exaggeration of this saying, it is as if He were replying, "Increase your faith? You already have some. Use it, and discover that it is like mustard, smallest of seeds, but able to become a great plant when allowed to grow." Faith is a faculty that develops in the using. Supremely, it is to be employed in answer to all we see in God, for by means of it we become linked with a higher power.

Here then is a faculty that has nothing to do with our good or bad qualities, nor this or that virtue. At last we can see how it comes into its own at great moments of religious awakening. *This* faculty is being asked for: not spiritual knowledge, understanding, wisdom, or fitness. Just faith.

> *All the fitness He requireth*
> *Is to feel your need of Him.*

Faith knows that need and where it can be answered. It can leap to accept all that God offers. It finds the way through while the "experts" and those who would climb to heaven by their own merit, or by their discernment of what they understand to be the rules, still wait to enter. "A man must start *beyond himself*," said Dr. Maurice Nicoll, "—and faith is the starting-point."

A recent Roman Catholic book indicates that a new breath is blowing over a wide area of Christian thinking on this subject. It admits, though carefully and with reserve, that during the Middle Ages "faith" was thought of almost entirely as "assent": i.e. when one "believed", one accepted the truth of the Gospel and the revelation proclaimed by the Church. Luther denounced this prevalent view. He had come to discover something deeper. What had come alive in his experience was also something to be found in Scripture. For him, indeed, it was based on Scripture. This book from a modern Catholic author[2] examines the relevant texts concerning faith in the Synoptic Gospels (there are thirty-seven of them) and admits in guarded fashion that though faith does mean assent to divine revelation, a paramount element in it is that of trust—the engagement of the personality in commitment.

In this diagnosis it is the "trust" aspect of faith upon which I am concentrating. The assent of the will and intellect to the truths of the Gospel is, of course, tremendously important: but this kind of "belief" can be given by the surface mind alone. If trust comes into operation then the deeper level of the personality must be engaged also. The whole-hearted support of the inner self (as the father of the epileptic boy knew: "Lord, I believe: help thou mine unbelief") is required, or otherwise faith wilts and fades.

There are times when we know we are called upon to take this leap into the unknown, or venture upon a course that at the moment seems contrary to the light of reason. We have heard God calling in the depth of our nature. The only light that shines is the kind of gleam we have come to recognize as from Him. What are we to do?

My wife has told me of a struggle she faced in an all-important week of the lives of both of us. I had written from the college, where I was training, to suggest our definite engagement. She tells me that the one stop in her mind had to do with the possibility, as a parson's wife, of being required to go abroad on the mission field. Because of home circumstances and other factors she was not prepared to do this.

While in this uneasy frame of mind she went to a missionary meeting in Manchester. It was addressed by a minister from Burma who introduced a petite Burmese lady to the assembly. By his introduction it was obvious that he thought he was the "attraction" of the evening. The Burmese lady, by comparison, was very small fry. Yet, said my wife, he did not realize that compared with what she had to give his contribution was as nothing.

With radiant face, the little black-haired woman spoke her first words. My wife has never forgotten them. "For me to believe in Jesus is to trust Him absolutely."

She went on to tell the gathering that when she was first asked to visit England, the idea seemed impossible. In those days Burmese women did not travel about their own country, let alone go abroad. "But," said she, "if Jesus wanted me to go, I knew He would help me." When she arrived at the boat—for her another new, and frightening experience—a missionary and his wife were there. They looked after her. And when she reached the shores of Britain, there was someone again to meet her.

Then came an unexpected catastrophe. Journeying to Manchester in November, amid the fog and damp, she lost her voice. This was on the Monday before the meeting on the following Wednesday. The doctor, hurriedly called in, prescribed various remedies and ordered her to stay in her room. What of her guidance? What of her sense of call?—her commission to these people in England?

"Please order a cab," she managed to squeak to her astonished hostess on the Wednesday, "I'm going to the meeting." "But you can't. The doctor says you must stay in this one temperature." "And what of Christ," she whispered, "who has said other things to me?"

Not until she took her seat on the platform did her voice return. And then, as my wife reports, she spoke in a beautiful bell-like voice, perfectly clear, heard by everybody in that large hall. Something about her spoke even more clearly, however, than her voice.

The result of this meeting upon my wife was electric. She had been praying earnestly for guidance. Now it had come. Her qualms about the future vanished. "For me to believe in Christ is to trust Him absolutely." Weren't the two of us to work for Him? Because of the witness of this Burmese Christian my wife, or future wife as she was then, felt able to trust herself more certainly to the power behind all things. For her this was a living moment of faith, as real as if the Lord Jesus had gripped her by the hand and looked into her eyes. The grip was within. And the answering trust came from the same quarter. We never went abroad—but that is another matter. The readiness was there, if need be.

Some people have to follow an empty path for a long time before coming to the discovery of what religious faith really is. They think of it as an intellectual matter and very little more. The struggle that led to the Reformation has thus to be refought in their individual experience. And it is not unknown for this to happen to someone who for years has taught in the name of Christ and spoken of faith countless times to others. When such a story is told with frankness we notice almost invariably that the missing element has been the attitude of trust. The Stranger Within has been kept out of sight and not been involved in what this person understands by faith. Tragically enough, the remedy is only discovered when some crucial happening breaks down the barrier that has been holding back this person from a real encounter with the Living God.

Against the unpropitious background of the first year of World War II a man called D. R. Davies published in Britain what proved to be a religious best-seller.[3] He continued to write, and his voice became well-known on British radio. When he died in 1958 he left behind the pages of an autobiography that recently has been issued.[4] It is an astonishing study of someone who emerged into leadership from pit-boy beginnings in South Wales. Without having discovered faith as we are discussing it here, nor having any ideas of the Stranger Within, he became minister of a church. Before more potent forces his lightly-held social gospel was soon whittled away, and his church transformed into what was virtually a socialist temple. Finally, spiritually bankrupt, he resigned.

Then Davies came to London in an effort to make a living by journalism. For some months he existed on the edge of starvation. Eventually, because of his oratorical gifts, he was taken up by one of the "Save Europe and Britain" movements of the time. Deeply read in Marx and Engels, the outbreak of the Spanish civil war engaged his deepest sympathies. He went to Spain and there saw something of the horror and futility behind that struggle. When he returned to this country it was as a broken and disillusioned man. To add to all his problems, his second marriage, which had begun with such high hopes, was by now a failure.

Walking by the sea one August night in 1937, Davies determined to end everything. He had reached the final point of despair. He plunged into the waves. It was then, he tells us, at this moment, when facing the abyss, that faith leapt alive in him. The enormity of what he was doing flared into his brain, and the reality and certainty of what God thought came home to him as well.

This, he tells us, was what made him give up his attempt at suicide, and clamber out of the water. Perhaps we, from outside his experience, would say that the shock of entering the sea, and the instinctive forces of self-preservation were decisive factors. Whatever it was, the inner gates opened, and the man who emerged knew himself as never before, and knew God in living power.

By means of this new-found faith D. R. Davies not only waded out of the water but climbed out of the morass into which his personal life had sunk. And not only did he win back his old place in the Christian Church, but found that he was able to speak with a new power that caught his generation. God had something to say through him—he was a minister indeed.

For D. R. Davies, then, as for many before and since, the moment he reached the end of his tether true faith was born, and the inner doors were unlocked. It would be true to say that for years he had been a man living on the strength of his own surface endeavours, trusting in his own powers and ability. God cannot enter some people's lives until, by the bitterest of experiences, they learn to put the deepest form of trust not in themselves, but in God.

Centuries ago a man who knew this uttered a cry which has since been re-echoed by thousands. It is known as the 130th Psalm. Martin Luther, having shared such an experience, wrote a poem:

> Out of the depths I cry to Thee,
>   Lord God. O hear my prayer!
> Incline a gracious ear to me,
>   And bid me not despair:
> If Thou rememberest each misdeed,
> If each should have its rightful meed,
>   Lord, who shall stand before Thee?

The last verse of this poem soars as in it the man of faith recalls how God has heard him, and recovered him in spirit. All God's people may know this, and must learn to put their real confidence and trust in His everlasting mercy:

Though great our sins and sore our wounds,
And deep and dark our fall,
His helping mercy hath no bounds,
His love surpasses all.
Our trusty loving Shepherd, He
Who shall at last set Israel free
From all their sin and sorrow.[5]

Richer Living

Thunder the brave irresistible message,
Life is worth living,
Through every grain of it.

W. E. HENLEY [1]

IN great moments of faith we leap to accept what God is revealing. We can do this all the more certainly because our steady, day-to-day attitude of trust in God provides us with a sure foundation beneath our feet. Our life has a settled positive purpose and is beginning to know true fulfilment. It has, at last, a sound basis. It is turned in a positive direction.

No one need explain to me what a "negative personality" is. I had my illustration when I was a boy.

The lady in question has long since passed on. It needs to be said that with her chronic negativism, she also possessed some most admirable qualities. It was for these her friends valued her. Those in her intimate circle had learned to turn a blind eye and shut their ears to the rest.

Since my mother came from the north, our house in London was often a rendezvous for the exiled sons and daughters of Scotland in our area. One of these was someone I shall call Mrs. Ferguson, a dyed-in-the-wool special Caithness brand of Scottish Calvinist. Her theme song, uttered in a voice heavy with gloom and resignation, was "What will be, will be." Invariably she was the bearer of bad tidings, and always the first to offer her own doleful brand of sympathy. It was meant well, but the effect was awful—especially upon small boys. Whenever I hear the expression, "Job's comforter" or "Wet blanket" I immediately think of Mrs. Ferguson, and hear her very tones as she used to say, "Ah well, we canna expect anything better. What will be, will be."

When you were ill, she brought you comforting stories of someone else who began exactly like you, whose illness progressed to something much worse, had to be hurried to hospital, only to die on reaching the operating table. However you felt before her arrival, your state was ten times worse by the time she left.

Her whole attitude was "negative" and depressing. Her husband, a wispy little man, had an innate toughness which must have been considerable. Fortunately for himself, his philosophy was of a different order. When his accompanying dispenser of woe appealed to him, "Isn't that so, John?", he had a neat way of turning the answer: "You say so, my dear."

How I wish that someone could have reached Mrs. Ferguson with a more Christian conception of faith. Her attitude was all the more firmly entrenched because she thought it honouring to God. If only this otherwise admirable woman could have been convinced of the damage she was doing! She attracted misfortune and trouble, and dispensed gloom wherever she went. For herself she was something like the old negro who used to say that if he survived February and March, he generally found that he managed until the end of the year!

Within my lifetime there has been a revolution in certain theological circles. The sombre Presbyterianism I knew in my early days—especially when as a boy of four I attended the interminable services in my mother's home town of Wick—has retreated, if not vanished entirely. The "fatalism" that was so characteristic an element is no more. In place of the unrelenting Judge, modern Presbyterianism presents the figure of a loving heavenly Father.

Everywhere there has been the infiltration, little or guardedly acknowledged, of an influence that has come in part from psychology. William James once made this comment, "The greatest revolution in my generation was the discovery that human beings by changing their inner attitudes can alter the outer aspects of their lives."

A whole philosophy has been built on this idea. It has encouraged a flood of "positive living" literature, of which the books of Norman Vincent Peale afford a notable example. There are even religious movements which have come into being because of this emphasis, as for example the "New Thought" type of organisation.

Sentences from the Bible like, "As a man thinketh in his heart, so is he," have sprung into prominence. Neglected Biblical teaching has been re-discovered, and, in particular, it has been noted how our Lord emphasised the importance of "inner" thinking and of the "positive" attitude to life.

If we watch the course of certain of our contemporaries we come to see that some lives seem to attract either success or disaster. It is as if the fear or the faith that is the dominant characteristic of such people draws towards them the very circumstances that help this characteristic still further forward. A sentence in the Book of Proverbs says, "The fear of the wicked it shall come upon him: but the desire of the righteous shall be granted." Again and again one has seen this demonstrated. Our popular ideas concerning a person's "luck"—either good or bad—have to do with this same phenomenon.

It was some time before I realised that what we are now considering is another facet of the Stranger Within and his outworking. It is from this inner centre that the new approach to life is asserted, and from there that this strange "magnetism" drawing the good towards us begins to operate. The positive approach of faith, of which we were thinking in the previous chapter, has been not just temporarily, but permanently, substituted for all other inner motivations. We have come to "trust the current that knows the way". This has become the settled disposition of the inner life. In place of fear and other destructive emotions, a radiant faith is ruling.

In another book[2] I have told the story of a man I have called David Dewars. I knew him well and with other people wondered at the way in which his life swung from failure and defeat to a most impressive Christian goodness. In place of his previous shoddy performances a new kind of success blessed him. One day he explained how the change occurred. Unexpectedly one Sunday morning he found himself in his old home church. He heard the preacher quote the well-known lines:

> *Ships sail East and ships sail West*
> *Wherever the winds may blow:*
> *For it's the set of the sails*
> *And not the gales*
> *That determine the way we go.*

The man sitting awkwardly in the back pew was reached by these words. Nothing else in the service mattered. David vowed that, under God, he would henceforth take a hand in setting his sails in a new direction. It meant all manner of costly changes, but, as he told me, it was a thousand times worth it.

David Dewars had to take decisions and to carry them through in the external world, but the real point of change was within. The metaphor of the sails, though it caught his attention, is not as exact a description of what happened as would be that of the setting of an inner gyroscope, or of a self magnetized to attract circumstances and conditions of a new order. Whenever we try to describe this inner motivation, we are bound to resort to metaphors and pictures. The dynamic fact that they cover is, however, that our lives are determined far more than most people realise by the "set" of our inner disposition. The mood that persistently dominates the Stranger Within, whether of faith or fear, affects the broad circumstances of our living to a great degree.

We possess a power of direction which can best be described in this metaphor of two opposite poles, "positive" and "negative". When we set this directing mechanism within us in the positive way, we find we are co-operating with God and life's forces.

An American scientist, who became well known for his discoveries, once applied this theory of attraction and repulsion to himself in a personal experiment. The circumstances in which this happened are most illuminating.[3]

At an age well over fifty this man was a "failure". There was no question about his innate gifts: he was a brilliant scientist. Yet life had gone sour. He was a social misfit, no one took any notice of his researches, and for no obvious reason he suffered constantly from chronic headaches.

Someone spoke to him about the difference between "negative" and "positive" living. To his scientifically trained mind, this seemed nonsense. However, as a scientist, pledged to the method of verification by experiment, it was put to him that he could not dismiss this important theory in so cavalier a fashion. So he promised he would conduct a personal experiment. He would deliberately set about altering the current of his thoughts and, in particular, redirect his inner life into new and more positive channels. When he found himself looking forward to an event with customary gloom, he would switch instead to a sense of confidence and pleasurable anticipation. He would not hold the thought that he was a "failure". God had given him gifts: they were to be used and recognized. All this was quietly done, within his mind.

After a time his scientific work began to gain the attention previously denied it, his social life was increasingly successful, and his headaches departed, never to return. Dr. Elwood Worcester, who tells us this, was present when, at the close of a scientific lecture, this now-famous scientist asked his audience to remain while he told them his story. Said this man, "I feel I have stumbled on a path of life." What had been begun as an experiment years before was now a settled habit of mind, resulting in richer, positive living.

It was our Lord Himself who uttered the sentence that summarizes the message of this chapter, "To him that hath shall be given, and from him that hath not shall be taken away that which he hath." Those who are receptive and welcoming shall receive more while the obdurate and the resistant lose what little of spiritual truth and understanding they may hold at the moment. This truth expands into all fields of living.

We are not trying here to find ways to exploit the forces of life to our advantage, nor to twist the will of God to serve our pleasure. We are discovering the path of life, the way of wisdom, the way planned by our heavenly Father which He wants us to find. We are deliberately turning the current of our life—thought, will and desire—towards God. We shall be looking for His goodness everywhere, knowing that by our new attitude we cannot fail to attract it. We are putting first the Kingdom of God and His righteousness, and in doing that we shall come to prove "all these things shall be added unto you".

This means that our inner self is being directed towards the light of life. Darkness results in endless wandering amid the kingdom of "dead ends", whereas the light shines on the way that increases unto eternal day.

12

Our Outgoing Influence

*Why are there men and women that while they are nigh
me, the sun-light expands my blood?*

WALT WHITMAN [1]

WE have been thinking of the power the inner self
possesses in determining life's direction, and in at-
tracting its circumstances and conditions. In this chapter
we look at a reverse consideration. Here we are concerned
not so much with the way that life answers us and our
attitude, but rather with our *contribution* to life—the
kind of influence we exert.

As well as continuing our exposition of the outworking
of faith in everyday living we are also overtaking two considerations at which we looked earlier. In Chapter 3 we
were thinking of the Sower-Seed-Soil relationship, and
noticing the way that certain people help to mould our
lives. Seed-thoughts lodge in the mind and work towards
a harvest, but they have far more chance to develop if the
sower happens to be someone greatly gifted with imagination and powers of persuasion, still more if he or she happens to be an admired personality. In this chapter we think
not so much of other people's influence on us as of ours
on them.

There was another chapter in which we noted the importance of "idle words" and unconsidered actions. These
often provide a better index to what we are than the mask
we turn to others. They are indications of the real self,
the Stranger Within. We now take that leading and its

implications a stage further. There is an even more subtle indication of the health of our inner self streaming from us into the life of the world: it is the outflow of personal power going forth completely unseen but devastatingly real, the kind of impression and influence one personality has upon another. This is reflected, of course, in our words and our actions, but even without them this personal influence is there. The question is of what nature is it?

One who knew Robert Browning said that to meet him for five minutes under a tree during a shower was to walk for the rest of the day with head held high and shoulders back.

There are people who make us feel better when we have been in their company. Life seems a finer thing for having known them. But there are others who affect us like a thunderstorm depression or the sight of the Black Country on a damp day.

We should remember that our lives touch countless others and they react to us as we do to them. This simple truth is not sufficiently recognized, but it is of fundamental importance.

Where can we pin-point the centre of this subtle effect we have upon others?

When we read this description of a man do we begin to find the answer? "I never met a man of purer spirit. His goodness seemed rather the spontaneous outflow of the heart than a conscious effort of the will. His courtesy, his humility, his unaffected goodness, his simple love of what is beautiful and good made his friends feel as if in his company they breathed a purer air." [2] It is the constitution of the inner self that determines the kind of influence emanating from us.

It is as if the inner life were like a spring from which waters flow—they can be either good or bad, sweet or bitter, wholesome or poisonous. Wordsworth reminds us of,

. . . that best portion of a good man's life
His little, nameless, unremembered acts of
kindness and of love.

These can be the outflow from that inner spring.

In the teaching of Jesus two pictures are given of what
flows from this source. One—the negative—is found in
parallel passages in Mark 7 and Matthew 15. Our Lord
comments that defilement begins not in failure to observe
external regulations, but in inward attitudes; and He continues His comment with a list of foul things that spoil
life—evil thoughts, adulteries, fornications, murders, thefts,
covetousness and so on. "All these," He states quite cate-
gorically, "come from within, and defile the man." In this
passage He is emphasising that what matters is not outward observance and appearance, but what is deep within.
There is the source of what issues into the life of the world.
Our Lord depicts the dreadful results of an inner life dark
with evil.

Fortunately we can set against this a passage which I
take to be its opposite. In John 7 our Lord refers to the
man who "believes on Him", which means someone to
whom Jesus is Lord not in word only but in deed and
truth: who is linked with Him in faith, who knows *His*
kind of love: the kind of person who has experienced the
invasion of the Holy Spirit, and whose inner life is therefore a fountain of good. "In the last day, that great day
of the feast," reports John, "Jesus stood and cried, saying,
If any man thirst, let him come unto me, and drink. He
that believeth on me, as the scripture hath said, out of his
belly shall flow rivers of living water." I have quoted this
passage as it is in A.V. where the phrase *epi tes koilias* is
translated literally as "out of his belly". It means, however,
just what we are considering.

Our phrase, the inner self, was unthought of by the Jews
of our Lord's day. The abdomen was pictured by them

as the seat of emotional life[3] and it is in this figurative sense that the expression is used. The New English Bible translates the phrase as "Streams of living water shall flow out from within him".

These two passages from Mark 7 and John 7 are in contrast: in one case we are given a list of horrible things coming from an unredeemed inner self, in the other we are shown beneficent streams of good flowing, all unconsciously, from the man whose inner life is stayed in God.

It is strange how little notice has even yet been taken of our Lord's insistence on the absolute priority of the forces hidden within man. The emphasis is always placed there —*within man*. Even as expressed in first-century phraseology and coming through the memory of only half-understanding disciples, we cannot miss it. In the beginning the disciples seem to have grasped very little of this element in His teaching. Only after the dramatic events of our Lord's Death and Resurrection and the coming of the Spirit in power did they really begin to understand.

Our Lord must have laboured endlessly to bring the point home. In Matthew's Gospel, especially, we can trace His concern to impart this principle. In the Sermon on the Mount our Lord insists that what matters in life and religion is not outward conduct so much as inner desires and passions. Adultery, murder and the rest are to be understood in terms of the inner motivations behind them. If you want good results you must have a good inner source from which they will flow. Make the tree good, said Jesus, if you want good fruit.

If the tree is bad then what is normal becomes abnormal and perverse. I have sometimes seen a great oak which has become diseased throwing out bulbous branches, soon to fester and decay. Quite normal desires become gross when allowed to grow out of proportion. The real person within is being consumed by an outrageous inner desire that is proving to be insatiable. Always the fruit coming from such a life is poisonous. The results are rank and offensive to others. Whilst prepared to welcome the manifestation of a healthy appetite, no one is happy if instead we are treated to an exhibition of overmastering gluttony and greed. Normal sex life, that finds its fulfilment in a true love relationship, becomes a foul thing if it deteriorates into licentiousness and lust.

In the middle ages casuistic theologians produced a list of the seven deadly sins. They were thought to be peculiarly "deadly" as compared with other sins of a more "venial" character. How they presumed to know this is a very interesting point of Church history. The list certainly betrays monastic origins. Pride, anger, envy, avarice, gluttony, lust and sloth. The list stands now, almost proverbially, for heinous and most regrettable personal conduct. There is certainly nothing out-of-date about the sins themselves. In the Protestant Episcopal Cathedral in Washington a piece of sculpture portrays these sins in modern setting. The figures are grouped round the central figure of Penance. Pride is caught halfway in a tumble while strutting vaingloriously forward; Envy, clad in rags, eyes a rich man's fur coat; Anger pounds furiously with his fists against the vaulting in which he is moulded; Covetousness, mute and abashed, carries the evidence of his theft; Gluttony, with face of revolting greed, gnaws at a bone and clutches a bottle; Lust is represented by a serpent entwining a man and woman standing amidst flames; Sloth is in his garden, asleep, while everything round him has wilted, except for the poison ivy creeping around his head. In all these cases something in itself normal and useful—a healthy self-respect, a desire for life's good things, an ordinary appetite etc.—has become abnormal and a source of offence.

These troubles, now as ever, are not to be dealt with on the surface, but within. That is their point of origin, and when we begin to track them down we discover the wisdom in concentrating not so much upon individual sins, as upon sin. Our enemy is not sins in the plural, but something in the inner self from which these manifestations spring.

It is impressive, again, to notice how little Jesus denounced actual sins. In the passage in the Sermon on the Mount where He speaks of some of them He spends His time tracing them to their roots. He is concerned about a complete redirection of our inner life. He comes to offer in Himself inner cleansing and renewal: a new way of living from within-outwards. His is the way of "wholeness" working from within.

You will notice that Paul in some of his Letters describes "sin" as if it were an evil force encamped within our nature. At times he uses the word "flesh" similarly. "It is no more I that do it but sin dwelling in me," he says. What he has discovered is an element in his inner self to which his conscious self now takes the greatest objection. He has located the place of defeat. Victory comes, as Paul asserts at the end of Romans 7, when we cry "Thanks be to God that giveth us the victory"—the victory is in Christ within us.

In this great Romans chapter Paul faces the dilemma of which we all know something: the tug-of-war between the two elements in our nature. Even though with our conscious self we have enthusiastically pledged ourselves to goodness, we can be defeated by the lurking and insidious enemy within. "The evil that I would not, that I do." This is the fearful thing. Small wonder that the apostle cries, "O wretched man that I am, who shall deliver me . . . ?"

This dilemma must be faced. It brings us to the same point as our Lord's teaching on the inner self. Viewed in one way, there is no more pessimistic teaching anywhere. We are to test ourselves and one another, said Jesus, by fruits. This is the way that a false prophet is unmasked. He will often deceive himself as well as other people. You cannot always judge by looking at him, nor by listening to what he says. He is in sheep's clothing, and can bleat like any ram. The test is that of final results and abiding influence—the test of fruits.

Applying this test, as the wise man will, not so much to others as to himself, suppose one finds something of the false prophet within oneself, what then? Good fruit from a good tree, says Jesus, corrupt fruit from a corrupt tree. Who can put the tree right? There seems no hope. The hope is alone where Paul found it.

Human beings may be likened to fruit-bearing trees and to inanimate objects in the realm of nature, but the likeness ends as soon as we reckon with the human being's power of self-direction and the ability to change. "I believe that man can change and go on changing as long as he lives," states Karen Horney. As soon as anyone recognizes himself as a false prophet or a corrupt tree, it need not be the moment of despair but the birth of hope. The recognition is the first part of a process which, under God, means transformation.

We have noticed the creative power of the realm within. We have observed that the origin of outward conduct can be traced to the inner self. We are aware, too, that our conscious mind acts as gateway, and in some measure as directive, to those forces deep in our nature. Thus we can consciously invite the Master of Life to enter our inner self, and deal with the things that are wrong. He is, in one sense, already there. What we must do is welcome Him and allow Him full control. Transformation can then happen, but it must happen at depth if it is to be positive and permanent.

Sometimes it needs a force of the fiercest character to effect this change. What dynamic, for example, must have been required to convert Saul the persecutor into Paul the Apostle. Pharisee of the Pharisees, Hebrew of the Hebrews, the force of an "*im*plosion" must have been needed. All the events contributing to this are charged with power. It might be said, looking back, that it needed every aspect of the martyrdom of Stephen to lead up to this complete change. Saul was present and never forgot what he saw and heard. Many of the touches in Acts 6 and 7 are those of an eye-witness: "his face as it had been the face of an angel," "crying, Lord lay not this sin to their charge." So strong was the influence that dying Stephen exerted upon Paul that the impossible became possible.

Within recent months Dr. W. E. Sargant has analysed some of the forces producing such apparently diverse states as "brain-washing" and religious conversion. To the embarrassment of some people he has discovered a number of factors common to both. But we need not be so surprised when we realize the upheaval necessary to bring the inner self to the point of such revolutionary change as conversion. Life has sometimes to do this savagely. It is only in this way that the apparently impossible can occur by which we can be swung from death to life.

If you are willing to allow yourself to be remoulded by the Master of Life, something can happen to you, and to the fruit you bear. The false prophet can become a real follower of the Lord. "Be transformed," said Paul, "by the renewing of your mind."

It is only when this process has gone deep that it has lasting effects. The reason why some "conversions" speedily fade is that they have not penetrated far enough, nor been absorbed by the whole being. The experience has been superficial, and this merely emotional transformation will not stand the strains in life's battle.

You remember our Lord's phrase: "a man's foes shall be they of his own household"? Doubtless these words were spoken out of His own experience. Loved ones and friends, because of their very concern for our safety and well-being, can sometimes hold us back from the path of vision or duty. But as one commentator suggests, the truth behind our Lord's words can be applied in a way still more intimate—the household in which a man's foes are found is that *within his own nature*. Often, in this sense, we are our own worst enemies. Our influence fails to be what we wish, not because of the failure of surface intentions, but because the stock of the tree is not good. Here, above all, we need to determine on a radical transformation for which we shall need our Lord's aid.

Deeper than ever we have known there must be an inner surrender to Him. Perhaps words like these begin to rise to our lips: "You know me, Lord, altogether, better than I shall ever know myself. Take control of these sources within me. Flood my inner life with Thy forgiveness. Fill it with Thy love and power. Come within and possess all my being."

I knew a man whose influence was once pernicious in the extreme. What came from him in those days when he was a communist medical student certainly did nothing to increase the stock of goodness in the world. Knowing him blighted at least one or two other lives. Someone said that he carried a poison-gas atmosphere about with him.

This unlikely person was taken to a Billy Graham rally in London. He went to scoff. He came away converted. And from that time the influence going out from his life changed, too. Not everybody knows his background now, nor needs to, but I know something of his work during these last eight years. When I met two young people from his church recently my memory recalled the "poison-gas" description. But these youngsters were full of enthusiasm for his leadership. "Just knowing Mr. So-and-so does you good," said one of them.

What would you have felt, I wonder, at such a moment? I was both elated and humbled.

Harriet Beecher Stowe, author of *Uncle Tom's Cabin*, must have marvelled many times at this miracle affecting the outgoing influence of people whose lives have been surrendered to Christ. In her poem *Abiding in Christ* there occurs this verse:

As some rare perfume in a vase of clay
Pervades it with a fragrance not its own,
So, when Thou dwellest in a mortal soul,
All heaven's own sweetness seems around it thrown.

Something of the beauty of Jesus begins to be seen in some of us who at one time were very far from Him. Our influence has to this extent been redeemed. And it has happened because He has come within our nature, casting out sin and filling the place with His glory.

Above all other gifts we should covet this possibility of Christlikeness emanating from within. This we seek not in mock piety, but in sincerity and reality. Christ in us is still "the hope of glory".

13

Love is the Key

> *Love is the key of life and death,*
> *Of hidden, heavenly mystery:*
> *Of all Christ is, of all He saith,*
> *Love is the key.*
>
> CHRISTINA ROSSETTI[1]

THE inner life is at its peak when we live by love—the quintessence of outgoing influences. "It is an experience of sharing, of communion," says Erich Fromm, "which permits *the full unfolding of one's inner activities*."[2] The further we enter into the divine adjustment the more we discover the importance of what Henry Drummond once called "The Greatest thing in the World".

It is impressive to notice that, at whatever level we look at life, love is a basic need. The source of our well-being and happiness is in loving and being loved. In this regard significant discoveries have been made in recent years in the field of child psychology. The importance of a "surrounding love relationship" in an infant's earliest days is now recognized and understood. Dr. Luther Emmett Holt had a recipe for ailing babies in his hospital. On their charts he wrote the following directions, "This baby needs loving every three hours."

As those babies grew towards manhood and womanhood they would need to learn that prescription's reverse side: not only do they need loving, but they must also *give* love. This is the sign of maturity. Life will not yield its satisfactions, nor come to fulness, if the need for receiving love is allowed to develop into self-centredness. And if outgoing love becomes perverted, developing into jealousy and hatred and other inverted forms—these in turn will decimate and destroy the life forces within. Whatever works against love is, by that token, a destructive agent in human personality and relationships.

With increasing love all the sensibilities are awakened. This is noticeable in any form of service. There is great force behind the work we do when the word "love" can be related to it. The talented musician who loves his art, and who loves people, is bound to be a better musician than one relying entirely on technique. The housewife loving her vocation brings to it a zest quickening all her home-making powers. Centuries ago Hippocrates wrote, "If a man wishes to be a good doctor, he must love his work and he must love his patients, must love all mankind."

In the development of this faculty there is again need for discipline. The boy feeling the call to become a doctor, musician, or engineer must first undergo training in order to perfect his craft. The more he is in love with what he is doing, the more he will be prepared to endure the tedium that will sometimes overtake him. Joyce Cary expresses this truth when he writes, "Love doesn't grow on the trees like apples in Eden—it's something you have to make. And you must use your imagination to make it too, just like anything else. It's all work, work."

So with the way of life we are exploring. For this divine adjustment the inner self needs all the aids outlined in previous chapters. The development possible in solitude and in the quiet of communion, the growth in faith, the joy of belief and certainty, the development in love and purpose, all help to make God's intention for us come true. In this there is no real tedium: only the joy of listening and obeying the faintest whisper of the One whom we love. When we love Him it is a joy and privilege to fulfil His will, and to seek every opportunity of communion and service. As soon as these tides begin to sweep into our life, there is hope. We are on the way to inner health.

Years ago, a remarkable woman, greatly respected through a large part of Lancashire, told her story to a friend of mine. She unburdened herself because of some rather fulsome praise that had come her way. "I haven't always been popular!" she confessed. "I'd developed into a really horrid woman, self-centred, and most unhappy. Nobody liked me. Because I snubbed their advances, the neighbours left me to my own devices. I habitually snapped people's heads off when they spoke. Then I became desperately ill, and as formerly, I was left alone. I'd no one to turn to. One day, through the open french window, a little girl came into the room. 'And where've you come from?' I managed to snap at her. 'I've come to see you,' she answered unperturbed. 'Yesterday at Sunday school the teacher told us that Jesus wanted us to be kind to horrid people. So I've come to see if I can help you.'"

For a moment the woman was nonplussed. Then she said, "Look, I'm very ill, and I do want help. Open the front door and ask your mother if she'd be good enough to come in." She did, and the mother, who was a Christian, helped this woman in her extreme need. More than that, mother and daughter bore with her unfriendliness, and love gave birth to love. The innocent goodness (and, at times, the naughtiness) of the five-year-old helped to melt a frozen heart and love was triumphant.

It is love that has the answer to all the problems of loneliness. The awful state of mind known by the would-be suicide vanishes when love enters and kindles response. It provides a new motive for living. The "I" within is able to surmount the difficulties that before seemed ready to engulf it. Life's wisdom is in the threefold relationship to which both Old and New Testaments direct us. We are to love God, and our neighbour and ourselves. Notice that proper love for the self is part of the commandment. "Thou shalt love thy neighbour as thyself." This kind of true regard for ourselves engenders proper self-respect. We seek our own highest welfare. This in turn becomes the guide to what we should seek for others.

Professor H. A. Overstreet has said that one of the insights that has come to us is that the capacity to love is something that has to grow. It is innate in us: but of all our talents, it is one often ignored and buried. Many an adult discovers it lacking in his nature. All the encouragements and exhortations to show love, to be loving, pass over his head. The ability has not yet begun to stir in his inner life.

If we find ourselves in the same position we must make a decision to begin. As with faith we learn to start with the seed. "If you have faith as a grain of mustard seed . . ." said Jesus. So here. Use what you have. Invest it. Employ it. Go ahead by fanning into flame the little spark of love that may be alight somewhere in your life. Develop it by using it. It is there at some point within your nature. Find it.

And remember that it is at this point that you come into contact with God. Look long at Jesus. Come to *know* Him. Through all that He is, and offers to us, He not only speaks of love, and offers us its shining example, but shares with us this spirit if we will have it. It is here that faith can aid us. By faith we begin to live on this basis, and so faith helps us to discover love.

Love enables us to understand other people, yet be tolerant. The Christian learns to love not with ulterior motive, but believingly and encouragingly. This means that we see people as they are and still more for what they may become. This is how God loves us.

We shall never win people from inner loneliness by answering their bitterness with our own, nor by arguing with them, nor lecturing them. There is only one way to help —to love them out of their unlovableness.

When I was a young man I happened to discover quite accidentally something of the power of outgoing love. A friend recommended a book then completely out of the range of my interest. I was fascinated by it. It was R. W. Trine's *In Tune with the Infinite,* which preaches a radiant kind of religion inviting one to a divine adjustment of life. The approach suggested was then new to me. What impressed me most was the idea that one could *let* Love into one's life. It was as if there were a sluice-gate somewhere in one's being that could be opened, and Love would come pouring in. One was invited to "experiment" with Love. Once knowing its power, it could be directed, almost as if it were a beam of light, upon other people for their good —and this completely without their knowledge.

At the time, I worked for a difficult employer, bitterly disliked by everybody under him. Would this operate in his case? I am amused now to think of myself when called into his office for a wigging, instead of inwardly rebelling, secretly turning this "beam of love" upon him. The odd thing, and I state this very humbly, is that it worked. Our relationships changed, and I would even dare to think that his attitude towards all of us in the office thawed a trifle. When I left he was most kind to me.

Something had happened to the young clerk himself. A barrier had been released. Where?—Within. I knew a little of what it meant to be "in tune with the infinite", and it hadn't happened in the world outside, but inside me.

It was in this way that I stumbled on the use of something which broke down barriers between people, uniting them, making friendship and fellowship possible.

In the years that followed I have been repeatedly impressed by those who possess this inner secret. One of the unpalatable facts ignored by R. W. Trine is that in a world like ours love often costs dearly. Concerned as it is with the best for others it has to meet with rebuffs and misunderstandings. It is not likely that it can continue without being challenged by suffering in some form or other.

I have watched parents exercising this spirit at the difficult stage of teenage rebellion, showing patience with what has often been downright rudeness and rejection. I have seen children continuing to show love to parents who have publicly disgraced them. I have watched the Prodigal's return. I have seen folk standing by while their loved ones themselves have had to suffer pain or indignity. And in all these and in so many situations like them, I have never ceased to marvel at Love. It sees things through. As Paul says, "It bears all things, believes all things, hopes all things, endures all things." But this is only true of deep, abiding love. Mere ephemeral concern, or surface attachment, does not stand up to the test.

Have you noticed that the symbol reminding us of the greatest Love known to this world is also the symbol of suffering? At the same time it is also the symbol of infinite power. We are in a world where love may be called upon to suffer, and it must be sufficiently strong to endure this. The more our innate capacity for loving is fulfilled and energised by the totally new capacity for love shown to us in Jesus, and shared with us by Him, the more strength our love will possess. This is "The Greatest Thing in the World".

In a previous chapter we referred to D. R. Davies. Through those same candid, autobiographical revelations he enables us to observe how this deep, abiding love grows not from the surface of our natures but from the inward realm with which we are dealing.

It was after he had reacted from the Church, and was given over to politics and socialism, that his second marriage took place. Davies tells us that he and his wife were head over heels in love. Their physical attachment was undoubted.

As the years slipped by and the time of his attempted suicide in 1937 approached, they were only keeping together, he frankly confesses, for the sake of their small daughter: this, too, in spite of the fact that their interests ran so much in harness. His wife was as ardent as he in efforts made for such causes as the People's Front and Spanish Aid. Davies says that, because of this, he has since come to see quite clearly that in itself identity of interests is not sufficient to keep a marriage alive.

A modern assumption is that love, when once it has died, can never be rekindled. Davies reports that he has lived to see that disproved, too. For when he passed through the experience recounted in a previous chapter, love returned and a new and deeper relationship began between his wife and himself. It is impressive to me that it is she who has seen this autobiography through the press, and has added her name to it in an opening word of explanation.

Here, then, is a clear case of someone in whom, late in life, faith came to birth, and to whom God revealed Himself: someone whose deeper nature opened and received God's love and forgiveness. On this new tide of life a deeper, more outgoing love was born. We can trace this to its origin. This love comes through the inner self, and it is what the New Testament refers to as the great possibility. It is God's love which, we are promised, will be "shed abroad in our hearts".

Of all the gifts that come into our nature there can be none greater than this. We must do all we can to open the sluice-gate within ourselves to let in this kind of enduring love. If there are barriers, we must seek to remove them. In prayer and meditation with Him we shall know what the obstacles are.

Says Paul in one of those great sentences of his, "To crown all there must be love, to bind all together and complete the whole",[3] or, as the Bishop of Southwell has translated this phrase, "Love is the unifying force of a fully developed life." This crowning, and unifying force must be sought as the continual goal of our ambition, and allowed to work from the very centre of our being.

As Kagawa used to say, the man who knows the tides of this immeasurable love surging within him knows for himself the power of God's love. Divinity is then dynamic within him.

14

Health and Healing

Only he who grasps the innermost nature of man can cure him in earnest.

PARACELSUS[1]

ACCEPTING that love is the key, we can go forward to unlock many fast-closed doors. Our life can become truer and freer in all its departments. This is so in connection with bodily health and well-being.

Every time we read a newspaper, or listen to a radio bulletin, we find confirmation of the principle that "the only news is bad news". There is no news value in the ordinary routine of a suburban street: but let one of the houses catch fire, one of the citizens commit murder, or bandits use the street for a mail-van robbery, then the place becomes a hive of reporters. Its fame, for a few hours at least, is assured.

It is because of this trait in human nature that when we turn to this topic of health and healing, most of us tend to think in terms of ill-health and stories of dramatic healing. Instead we should remember that for the majority the great proportion of their earthly days are lived in a state of remarkably good health. When we take a holiday, or journey to some new place, it is worth taking a look at the folk with whom we come into contact. How well they are, and how full of enjoyment of the ordinary things of life. And when we are healed from illness, it usually happens with a complete absence of anything approaching the dramatic. We find our way back quietly to normality.

The Creator's purpose is that we should be well and happy. This is life's normal state when all is functioning efficiently. We can say that this is God's intention for us, and we can be sure about this since we see it exemplified in the life of Jesus, and observe it equally in the love and compassion with which He regarded those in ill-health. He saw it as part of His function as Agent and Revealer of God to put this wrong right. We need to remember that the Jewish view held illness and suffering as punishment for sin. Our Lord's concern was to make men healthy in every department of their living.

Health, said a doctor talking to a group interested in the Christian viewpoint, is more than the perfect harmony and equilibrium of the bodily organs, more than a rhythm of work and rest, more than the quick response of body to mind, and adaptability to external circumstances. It is more than the state of well-being when we are usually unaware of our bodily functions (only when we are ill do we begin to notice our heart-beat, our breathing etc.); and more than the mere absence of disease. To the Christian, said this physician, health is something dynamic, infectious, outgoing. In this case it is not an end in itself but a state of being a fit channel for the life of God to enter and flow into the life of the world. His Love can then express itself through this level of our being, as well as all others.

In this chapter we look at the rôle of the inner self in relation to health and sickness. As in all the other matters we have been examining, it is the Stranger Within that has far more to do with our relative health or ill-health than is ordinarily supposed. It is generally accepted that "Brother Body" when ailing can drain all the happiness out of life and depress the best of us. The reverse truth—that the self within has a very great deal to do with the state of our total health—has not so often been accepted.

One of the major changes of our time is the way medical science has come to recognize this latter fact. Scarcely a book written about these matters today does not refer to "body-mind relationship". What is known as Psycho-somatic medicine is now a most important branch of medical research and practice. The *materia medica* were once very material indeed. For centuries healing was a matter of physical remedies—plasters, balms, medicines, crutches, massage, surgery etc. By the help of these, and sometimes despite them, bodies recovered a large measure of health. The *materia medica*, ever developing in efficacy and of enormous value, will always be of the greatest importance. But other factors concerning man's inner nature are increasingly being studied and taken into account by surgeons and physicians. Hospital practice is gradually recognizing these new principles.

May I share with you a story that helped to convince me of the important relationship between the inner self and total health?

In the years when I was working with my medical friend, a patient aged sixty was introduced to him suffering from a strange complaint—"gallstones that aren't there". For some time the patient had been experiencing acute pain. Although an operation had proved the gall-stones non-existent, the pain persisted.

At the time my friend was interested in the recently published account of the gall-bladder researches of two Viennese doctors, Oeschler and Wittkower. They had conducted a series of experiments, first on animals and then, by means of hypnosis, on human patients, by which they established that the secretion of bile is affected by strong emotions. When the humans were given sugges-tions causing joy, sorrow and anxiety the flow of the bile was increased from twice to six times its normal quantity. This was interesting enough, but what was remarkable was the fact that *annoyance* had precisely the reverse effect. When this emotion was intense the bile stopped instantly. Not until the emotion had subsided, and the patient recovered equanimity, did the natural flow begin again.

Having studied these experiments, my friend asked his patient a number of questions that must have surprised her. They seemed to have no connection with her trouble. What have family relationships to do with a pain in the gall-bladder? The sequel showed how much they had to do with the physical trouble.

Having won the patient's confidence, my friend discovered that she was most disturbed at the attention her husband was bestowing on another woman. She had not wanted to show this annoyance, but the situation had become so unbearable she felt she must leave him. "You haven't left him, however?" "No," replied the patient, "I couldn't." "This," said the doctor, "is the source of your mental conflict. You want to leave him, and you don't want to leave him; and you are paying for this in your body."

At first the woman accepted this diagnosis very dubiously. The doctor had to convince her of the force of body-mind relationship. This he was able to do by quoting other cases. Within a short time the patient began to realise the truth for herself. Her treatment included a bottle or two of virtually harmless medicine, but the real cure lay in the talks with the psychiatrist about the home situation. She was given suggestions how to unravel the domestic tangle. She made herself much more attractive, waking from the sleep of dowdiness into which she had drifted. She went with her husband to social functions, and within a short time the "other woman" vanished from the scene. And while all this was happening, the pains that had bothered her for so long disappeared. The bodily-secretions, upset by suppressed rage and frustration, returned to normal once harmony within was restored.

When the body is sick there are various agencies that can help. We can think of them on three levels: material, mental and spiritual. Remembering what we have already stressed regarding the interaction of our life in all its phases, the best possible cure is often a compound of the three. Because we have been underlining the importance of the inner self, and therefore of spiritual and mental factors, we must not give the impression that we minimise the importance of the physical. To do that would be to make the same mistake as old-time materialistic medicine.

Entities such as germs and bacteria have physical existence and when encountered by the body have definite effects. The white corpuscles of the blood, the defending army of the lymph, fight their battles against these intruders, and the battles are material enough—as are the results of either winning or losing. Our very life at times depends upon their destruction.

It must be mentioned, with due concern, that some people come into the world with an impaired constitution or with weak or deficient organs. Others sustain accidents, or receive wounds. Limbs are broken, bodies injured. All these are possible happenings in a material world. Worst of all, however great faith a man may possess, there are certain facts about the physical body that seem to be final: as is evidenced when we see a fellow creature with one arm or one leg. But I am sure our study will show that such a handicapped person may find new life which can be more than compensation for his physical loss. Life is full of examples.

I have mentioned the instance in which my psychiatrist friend cured a condition of physical pain in the gall-bladder. The cure had psycho-somatic overtones. But for this one case involving relief by mental and spiritual processes, it must be remembered that there are thousands where pain in the gall-bladder has *physical* origin, requiring medicine, sometimes surgery, to remove the obstruction.

One of the most remarkable research projects in the

history of medicine was that reported in 1947 by Professor Hans Selye of Montreal. After a series of experiments, he established that the body has a unified defence mechanism against disease. This operates through the glands.

We know for ourselves the immediate reaction set up in the body when we are afraid or violently angry. What is happening is that the adrenal glands are pouring their stimulating hormones into the blood stream. By this means extra sugar is released and is available in the blood to lend power to the muscles. We have watched people's faces go white. The pupils of the eyes dilate. We know ourselves the typical reaction to apprehension by having "butterflies" in the stomach. For the moment energy is directed to the places where it will be most useful either for flight or fight, and diverted from other parts of the body, i.e. from the face and stomach, where it is not immediately required. Notice that this happens *instinctively*. We cannot prevent such reaction. Our bodily defence system is built on this pattern. There is a similar glandular reaction when germs invade us, or we are threatened by disease.

When we are in a state of health, the delicate balance of these various hormone secretions is maintained. But Hans Selye proved that when we endure strain of an intense order then trouble can eventuate because glandular reaction becomes disorganized. The flow of one or other vital hormone is interrupted.

He also emphasized that this disorganization can result either from external conditions, such as biting cold, searing heat, exposure to germs, injury; or it may have its origin in the world within, in fear, anxiety, or some other emotional disturbance. The disruption can come from either direction.

In a number of diseases, which since Selye's researches are called "stress diseases", immediate aid can be given by supplying deficient hormones by means of medicine or injection. But if the condition of stress has its origin in the inner self then this is mere ambulance work, affording only temporary relief. What needs to be corrected are the reasons for the emotional disturbance. It is the inner self that must be treated.

Even the troubles that attack us from without receive either encouragement or rejection according to the state of the inner being. Also some of us have "a vested interest in ill-health". Our real self sometimes accepts a defeatist policy towards life and unconsciously works towards illness. Prof. Selye in his book *The Stress of Life* states, "our failure to adjust ourselves correctly to life-situations is at the very root of the disease-producing conflicts."

The most important adjustment is that between our-selves and God. When this divine adjustment is made then so much previously wrong within is automatically set right.

Do you recall the words our Lord used on several significant occasions? "Thy faith hath saved thee; go in peace." He said this to the "woman who was a sinner" in the story given in Luke 7. We are told that her sins, which were many, had been forgiven. This was a spiritual and mental cure. Her mind was set at rest. Jesus used exactly the same formula when the injury was working out in bodily terms. To the woman who "touched Him" in the crowd He declared, "Daughter, be of good comfort: thy faith hath made thee whole; go in peace." And to the Samaritan, one of the ten cured from leprosy, and to Bartimaeus, receiving his sight, His words were much the same.

The original Greek word *sesōke* in these passages is translated in the King James version sometimes as "saved" and at others "made whole". This word was used by writers of that time to describe restoration to physical health and strength. The Bible word "salvation" is derived from the same root. Wycliff invariably translates the latter word as "health": so that in the Zaccheus story, "This day has salvation come to this house" becomes "This day has health come to thy house". A man had come to know the divine adjustment deep within him. He was able now, through Christ, to enter into fulness of living.

We cannot deserve, earn, merit, or "buy" salvation. It is God's gift to all who ask. By means of it we are brought into fellowship with Him and His will. On the physical level this implies the prospect of full bodily health. Our faith links us with God in living power. Our Lord was drawing attention to this when He used the words, "Your faith has saved you". Faith, as we have seen, is a dynamic act opening the deepest part of our nature to God. By means of it we accept what He is offering us in living power. Then suddenly or gradually we are brought into wholeness —into health.

In my early ministry I was appointed to a group of churches in South West London. One of my colleagues, an older man, had for years been thinking and reading about spiritual healing. He felt he ought to institute some form of service at which prayers might be said, and sick people anointed with oil, after the pattern James mentions in the 5th Chapter of his Epistle: "Is any among you sick? let him call for the elders of the church; and let them pray over him, anointing him with oil in the name of the Lord: and the prayer of faith shall save him that is sick, and the Lord shall raise him up . . ."

He held back from doing this, not so much from fear of incurring the disfavour that is the lot of all pioneers, but because he felt unworthy. The issue was finally forced on him.

Some of the young men of the church came to him in deep distress. One of their number was under sentence of death from cancer of the throat. The doctors had done all possible, but there was no hope. What could they do to help their friend? They mentioned the name of Leslie Weatherhead, who had recently come to London. Could they ask for his aid in this case? My colleague told them that Mr. Weatherhead, as he was then, only dealt with "functional" and not "organic" diseases. So insistent were these men that my colleague finally arranged a healing service, at which they and their friend were present. In a spirit of deep concern, and in great faith, they prayed together and anointed him. He recovered. Within a few months he was speaking in the name of Christ in open-air services.

Twenty years later, I returned to South West London to work in the same group of churches. The young man who had had cancer was now a steward, and his minister was a successor to the colleague of whom I have just written. He, too, was intensely interested in spiritual healing.

It seemed the greatest tragedy when this second minister became ill. He asked for the prayers of the Prayer Group he had formed, but the illness was not arrested. There came a time when he *had* to go to hospital. The glands in his neck and shoulder had developed to such an extent that he was in danger of being suffocated. His trouble was cancer of the lymphatic glands, and the prognosis was grave. One night he was moved from the general to a specialist hospital. On this occasion, there was imminent danger that he would literally be choked to death.

He had gone into hospital, however, not in defeat but in a spirit of serene faith that deepened with every day. He submitted to the X-ray treatment and co-operated with every suggestion made by the specialists and the hospital authorities. There is a further link with the previous story in that Leslie Weatherhead, who knew him well, asked for the prayers of the City Temple congregation. A large circle by now were praying for him. The minister himself asked to be prayed for, not in the spirit of defeat, but of victory. He wanted people to concentrate on the thought of Christ's power to bring wholeness. In their prayers they saw him whole and able to do the work to which God had called him.

To the surprise of many who had not shared in the prayers nor the faith, he emerged from hospital well on the road to recovery. After a period of convalescence he was able to resume the full work of his ministry, and is now serving in a very difficult post. He himself ascribes his cure to the double efforts of medical care and of prayer and faith. His own sense of peace with God and fellowship with Him deepened enormously as a result of this experience.

"God's agencies of healing are manifold," says this man. "The thing to remember, however, is that they are *all* God's."

Those who have come to know the inflow of God's Spirit into their lives, and who have experienced His forgiveness and been prepared to deal with all the barriers within their nature, are people whose lives are greatly reinforced. When faced with sickness, or disaster, they can tap these spiritual resources to meet the emergency. Healing power flows swiftly to their aid. They are not dominated by fear or restlessness: nor do they give way to stress and strain. They are able to overcome adverse conditions through the certainty of God's presence and power.

Yes, God does heal.

15

Release

*It is only on an inner plane that we can outgrow the bonds
of the past, see it with new eyes and forgive it. And a
past forgiven is no longer a liability but an asset.*

HUGH L'ANSON FAUSSET[1]

IN the last chapter we noticed that the condition of
health and happiness is meant to be normal. Stress
disorganises and ill-health and unhappiness result. For a
return to wholeness obstacles must be removed. What
follows in this chapter is really in continuation of this
teaching as well as a follow-up of our consideration of the
place of Love in the Christian life. I want to stress the
point about inner barriers because they obstruct the entry
of Love into our lives, as well as preventing bodily healing.
The matter is linked with the consideration of pride and
resentment. And forgiveness is so important that space
must be given to it.

Think then of some of the barriers preventing us from
knowing the in-flow and out-flow of Love. All of them are
impediments to the enjoyment of God's health-giving
powers. The unforgiving spirit is one: so are hatred and
anger, enmity and vengefulness: so is an unresolved sense
of guilt; so are anxiety and fear. The list is long: resentments, jealousies, prejudices and bigoted dislikes, these are
but a few. They block our full vigour, both spiritual and
physical. The divine adjustment we seek demands that
these be dealt with in our inner being.

Consider how the world is bedevilled with resentments.

Folk feel injured when they imagine they are not given their seemingly rightful place in society. They become resentful when comparing their intellectual ability, or their situation or their appearance, with others. They suffer from real or fancied injustice. You have only to look at the faces of people who have been feeding on these false emotions to see what has happened. I recall one man whose mouth was twisted into a permanent sneer. When the grace of God began to work in him, his features gradually lost their sardonic twist, and a warm smile took its place. Love was at the centre of his life in place of hatred.

A number of physicians claim that resentment is intimately related to many of the blood pressure and heart troubles which abound. Smouldering resentment also results in dyspeptic complaints. Dr. Stanley Jones tells of a woman who said to him, "I lived with my son-in-law for five years under the greatest tension. At the end he had a stomach ulcer, and I had arthritis. We separated, and both got well."

The records of the Cornell University Medical College include detailed accounts of a series of experiments with hives, a blotchy skin disorder accompanied by intense irritation. Thirty patients who suffered periodically from this complaint were picked at random. They were carefully examined to see if there was any emotional background to their case. It was discovered that when a personal problem was discussed the skin of the patient reacted immediately. In every one of the thirty cases the basic problem was resentment. The patients believed themselves unjustly treated at home, in sport, or in business. When this resentment was artificially stimulated instruments showed that minute blood vessels in the skin became dilated, bringing on an attack of hives. It was as simple as that.

For the sake of our health, both inner and outer, we must determine not to cherish resentments. This does not mean that we shall pretend not to have been injured when we have. But we simply face the fact and deal with it. By God's grace we must try to understand the person who has harmed us, and to learn the way of human sympathy and of good humour. The more we understand the workings of the inner self, the more we shall be able to appreciate one another. "Let not the sun go down upon your wrath," counselled Paul in one of his shrewd shafts of wisdom. Get the poison out of your system before you go to bed. Whatever you do, don't give it time to get into your inner self or else you will suffer.

Booker T. Washington, the American negro, had the right approach to this problem. Said he on one famous occasion, "No one shall ever narrow or degrade my soul by making me hate him." Dr. G. W. Carver, whom we have already mentioned, used to cool irritated coloured students by advising them, "Even the most unfriendly criticism may be a help if you take it rightly." He himself demonstrated how the spirit of good humour can prevent the seeds of resentment from obtaining deep roots. A number of his biological students thought they would make merry at his expense. They presented him with a curious creature concocted from the body of a beetle, the head of an ant, the legs of a spider, and the antennae of a moth. "We've just found this strange bug, Professor. What is it?" After due examination came the laconic reply, "This, gentlemen, is what I think we would call a humbug." Yes, resentment is humbug and to be laughed at!

If it should be that we have been harbouring grudges and resentments, then what we must do is not to fight them, but surrender them. Let them go, swallowed up in the Love of God. He can deal with them in a way we never can.

Our Lord introduces us to a positive way of living, reversing these destructive emotions. "Love your enemies," He commands, "pray for them that despitefully use you and persecute you." In His own immortal example, He shows and shares this spirit with us. We are to believe this, accept it, and live by it. As God in Christ forgives us we must learn to forgive others. This is the spirit of Love.

I remember listening to a woman saying of her son, "He never forgives". What a tragedy—for him, as well as for those with whom he lived and worked.

Our Lord emphasized the problem of the unforgiving spirit, and made sure His teaching would be remembered. It is inserted in the heart of His pattern prayer: "and forgive us our trespasses as we forgive them that trespass against us." In Matthew's account of the Sermon on the Mount the prayer is followed by this unequivocal statement: "For if ye forgive men their trespasses, your heavenly Father will also forgive you: but if ye forgive not men their trespasses, neither will your Father forgive your trespasses." The point receives further stress in the story of the Unforgiving Debtor whose large debt was cancelled, but who straightway went out and took by the throat his fellow servant who owed a comparatively paltry sum, refusing his plea for mercy, and having him thrown into prison.

You cannot be forgiven, if you will not forgive. No amount of visible action compensates for the forgiving spirit, which comes from within. "If thou bring thy gift to the altar, and there rememberest that thy brother hath aught against thee; leave there thy gift before the altar, and go thy way; first be reconciled to thy brother, and then come and offer thy gift." The true reconciliation can only be effected by a change of heart and outgoing Love.

"How many times shall my brother sin against me, and I forgive him," asked Peter, "until seven times?" His Lord answered, "I say not unto thee until seven times but until seventy times seven." Whatever the provocation our spirit must ever be ready to make the forgiving gesture.

We must learn even to forgive ourselves. This is a lesson some people find very hard. Years ago I came across such a case. Placed far too soon in a position of trust and responsibility, a nineteen-year-old girl was involved in a financial fraud. Life thereafter became intolerable. "How could I have done those things?" was her ceaseless question and reproach. One night she threw herself from the High Level Bridge into the River Tyne, determined to end everything. She was seen and rescued, half-drowned and hopelessly weak. Many kinds of treatment followed, but the crux of her cure was centred in finding release. She had to be brought to the point where she would accept God's forgiveness, and then forgive herself. This she did.

Starr Daily, the converted criminal, whose books have helped so many, tells how he was once accosted by an ultra-pious lady who said: "I suppose you suffer terribly because of your sinful past as a criminal." What a tactless, stupid remark. And how wrongly does it interpret God's way with us. The forgiveness of God is real. Its power releases us from the bondage into which our past mistakes have forced us. Starr Daily has accepted this, and lives now by the strength of it. He rightly says, "If I sat around brooding in self-condemnation over a past which has been forsaken, and which I cannot change now, then God would give me no power in the present to help myself and others." If we would enjoy the forgiveness of God, we must learn to forgive ourselves.

One of the great words, and great philosophies, for the Christian is the way of "acceptance". We are not to confuse this with "resignation", a grace which few would wish to defend. "Acceptance" is constructive working with the forces of life as we discover them. "Grant us the wisdom," says a well-known prayer, "to alter what can be changed, to accept what cannot, and the wisdom to know the difference." And among the things which must be accepted is the entail of the past. Some of its results will go on.

We recognize that, but we are not meant, for that reason, to carry the bitterness and guilt of the past about with us. God's great gift of forgiveness obliterates these. The things with which we cannot deal are engulfed in the tide of His almighty love and power. Anxiety and tension must go. We forgive the past, consenting anew to life as it is, and as it can be, in God.

John L. Casteel[2] tells of a young woman who had committed a number of indiscretions before marriage. After marriage these weighed on her conscience, giving her no peace. Seeking her minister she poured out her story. Again and again she came. "I'm paying the price for my sins," she reiterated. What she meant was that her marriage was childless, and this she interpreted as God exacting retribution for her past. In the midst of one of these acts of self-confession, which were rapidly becoming orgies of self-pity, the minister cut her short and said, "Believe me, Eleanor, your sins *are* forgiven." This was said powerfully and authoritatively. Some weeks later a radiant man and wife came to see him with the news that their first child was on its way. God was most certainly not exacting retribution! This story provides a powerful example of the way life's creative forces can be held back by factors that have become barriers within the inner self.

God offers us a new way of living. It must however be received and entered into, under His conditions. What are blockages and impediments must go; and their places taken by the positive inflow of God's Love and Peace, which in turn act as powerful antidotes. "Let the peace of God, which passeth all understanding, stand sentinel over your hearts and minds in Christ Jesus." That is the meaning of what Paul originally wrote in those familiar words of benediction. This peace of God, which is something far beyond our power to understand, will stand guard over our inner nature, if we will but let it. This is the promise, and the possibility. *Let it happen*, counsels Paul. The barriers that once obstructed the flow of God's goodness into our lives disappear, and are replaced by a force which guards against their return.

So we come to the spirit of "acceptance" and co-operation, knowing now the unimpeded tide of God's love and power, making our lives whole and useful.

We are released and can begin to rejoice in the discovery of true freedom. Ahead of us is the possibility of a balanced life with full development of character and potential assets. We are free to live in God's world in the way that He intended.

16

Safeguards

Many are deceived in the end, who at first seemed to be led by the Holy Spirit.

Thomas á Kempis[1]

BY prayer, positive living and direction, by inner cleansing and renewal we have been moving towards the goal God has set before us in Christ. This chapter is written with affectionate concern. To give adequate direction it is necessary to be absolutely honest in counsel. Now, as we realise a depth of love and service hitherto impossible beckoning us in Jesus, and are invited to know the invasion of the Spirit, we must pause.

Here we consider some of the dangers besetting our path. They are very real, though we may think it unlikely that we shall be attacked by them. If we are too sure of this, perhaps in that lies our greatest danger. Let him that standeth, counselled Paul, take heed lest he fall. Especially would it be wrong for us to neglect some of the warnings and safeguards coming from our Lord Himself.

* * * *

When Jean Sibelius was fifteen he began to study the violin. Hitherto as he wandered through his beloved Finland he had been at a disadvantage. Again and again he had wanted, watching some beautiful scene, to express his feelings in music. All he could do, as he found himself thinking of a tune, was to wait until he could reach home and reproduce it on the piano.

But with his violin he was liberated. He liked to take it with him on summer rambles so that whenever he felt inspiration, he could express it. Summers spent at Sääksmaki were memorable for the concerts he played to the birds from a platform of rock overlooking Vanajavesi. When he went sailing at Lovisa he often stood in the bows with his violin, improvising to the sea. The composer of *The Swan of Tuonela* and *Finlandia* had begun early to marry his music to the beauty of his native land.

That picture of the young Sibelius finding release and a way of expression speaks of the importance of bringing together two realms: the within and the without—what comes to us by way of inspiration and what is there in the "given" world outside. This introduces the complicated relationship between what is "subjective" and "objective". By subjective I mean that which has its origin in our personality and by objective that which is external and exists in the outside "given" world.

We need to see with utmost clarity that the way to God through the realm within is not a trick, a new gimmick, a shibboleth. It is the way of rightness, or righteousness: of thorough integration leading to wholeness, or holiness. What we feel within ourselves and express in various ways through our words, our actions, and our nature, must be brought into correspondence with the great outside world of reality in which we live. This world of reality is not our creation. Our subjective ideas must harmonise with it. That is what is meant by living in accordance with the truth.

In this book we have been laying stress on the subjective realm within. Like all other wisdom regarding our living this needs balancing with complementary truth. There are dangers, and very serious dangers, in too intense a subjectivity. We need to look at some of them.

One peril is that we shall forget that we are but the *channel* of the power and inspiration flowing through us.

I have said there is a "fountain life" possible for us, whatever our state. This is so, but when we begin to know it, we make the mistake of forgetting that God revealed this and guided us to these springs. Our inspirations, thoughts and impulses are sometimes accepted as our own creation. Our ego becomes inflated, our sense of power perilous.

"I am the vine: ye are the branches," said our Lord. There is always the risk that we shall overlook this. Our life consists in remaining with Him: apart we die—or the life languishes deathward.

What a shock it is to realise that there are dangers which can overtake not only the lukewarm, but those enthusiastic in their religion. Their very enthusiasm can carry them away prematurely in their own strength. Then there are the troubles resulting from the over-excited ego. Knowing but a little of the power at the heart of life, some people are inclined to be swept into a burst of self-glorification.

We all know of churches "run" by one man; and of women whose influence, though tremendous, is often pernicious in defeating the Church's true work. We have seen egotism exposing itself in those who, held back at home or feeling insignificant at business, make the Church a sphere in which to exercise petty power. These are familiar illustrations of something which, occasionally, works out in much greater measure. We may not fall into the errors suggested, but some of us may have tripped.

Early in Christian history Montanus of Phrygia led a movement meant to quicken the Church's slumbering life. He had been a priest of Cybele. The Phrygian region was an area where cults abounded that sought escape from the burden of mortality through ecstasy. Montanus and his prophetesses claimed to be mouthpieces of the Holy Spirit. What they said, therefore, was thought to supersede the earlier Christian revelation. His enemies declared that Montanus actually claimed, "I am the Father, the Word and the Paraclete," and Maximilla, one of the prophetesses, "I am the word, and spirit and power."

Ronald Knox's large work entitled *Enthusiasm* (in which he uses the word in its 18th century connotation concerning extravagant and unnatural religion) and Roy Strachey's *Fanaticism*[2] afford a number of instances of similiar aberrations occurring throughout Christian history.

In England in the 16th century, Thomas Nayler, converted by the preaching of George Fox, sold his farm, left wife and family, and became a roving Quaker evangelist. Unfortunately he allowed a Messianic Legend to grow up around him. After standing trial before a Committee of the House of Commons for his pretensions, he was pilloried, and before imprisonment whipped through the streets, branded on the forehead, and his tongue bored through. We are not concerned here with the savagery of this punishment but with the nature of Nayler's offence.

In our own day the negro leader known as Father Divine makes the most astonishing claims concerning himself, and thousands of his followers, having given him all their possessions, think of him as god.

Since the days of Paul the Church has been plagued with what is known as the Antinomian heresy. We have been delivered by Christ from the "law" and promised complete forgiveness. We can use this then, say the Antinomians, as a kind of ceaseless credit against which we can draw with all the licence of our natures. "Let us sin that grace may abound."

Those who discover the importance of the realm within are drawn into similar dangers when they overrate the importance of the mental and spiritual as against the physical and material. The life of man as we have noted is a unity, in which all parts of his nature are balanced. Christianity is an incarnational religion. What issues from within expresses itself in terms of the bodily life. Some mystics, however, have not seen this clearly. What is physical and material is denigrated, and sometimes thought of as antagonistic to God. When men come to think like this the body tends either to be maltreated and ignored, or to be given over to all manner of self-indulgence. St. Francis of Assisi had a very happy way of expressing the truth when he used to speak of *"Brother* Body".

Then there have been those who have sought the invasion of the Holy Spirit by casting themselves into some form of hysteria. An instance of this kind of extravagance is found in the 18th-century Convulsionaries of France. Their practices seem akin to those of Mohammedan dancing dervishes. After ceremonies inducing trance and hysteria, with men falling like epileptics while others twirl, dance and caper, shrieking and groaning at the same time, they would suffer bodily injuries that would have severely wounded normal people. Sword cuts and injections with sharp points and lancets would be undergone without bleeding, and bruises and contusions received without complaint.

Roy Strachey's book is especially valuable in that it includes the notes made over a long period of years by Hannah Whitall Smith, the Quakeress and author of the once popular *Christian's Secret of a Happy Life*. The notes concern folk in *modern* America who have been led into extravagance and disaster. Mrs. Whitall Smith knew those two extraordinary men Thomas Harris and Laurence Oliphant. Their stories which began in intense spiritual searching ended in flagrant immorality. So many instances came to her notice of people who in their quest for mystical experience fell into pitfalls connected with sexual ecstasy. Looking for thrills and raptures they became easy prey to these terrible errors.

One of her warnings concerns people who believe that all interior impressions coming to them in sacred and solemn moments must necessarily be of God. On this matter she writes, "I cannot tell how many fanatics, when I have tried to convince them of their errors, have said to me: 'But, Mrs. Smith, what *am* I to do? These inward voices come to me in my most solemn and sacred moments, when I feel myself to be nearest the Lord and most abandoned to Him, and how can I believe that at such moments He would allow the delusions of the devil to deceive me?'"[3] In giving themselves up to the guidance of these interior voices, without regard to the teaching of Jesus or the fundamental principles of the Bible, and without reference to the loving, forgiving, believing community of Christ's people, they are on a path fraught with danger.

Always there is the risk of private judgment and unconscious motives, personal prejudices or whims masquerading as spiritual guidance. This is not a new peril: but it is one concerning which we need to be on guard. We must remember that our Lord promised that we should always know His voice. Equally we should know our own voice when it is trying to pass itself off as His. It is a matter of maintaining spiritual integrity. In this there must be absolute honesty.

Mrs. Whitall Smith writes of the infectious nature of suggestions concerning divine guidance and relates how a member of a circle of "seekers" passed on a most inane suggestion which all of them copied in turn, until one person strong-willed and sensible enough, stopped it and broke the chain.

She also declares that you cannot reason with people far gone in a fanaticism. My own experience has proved this statement. I once became the object of attention of a group of Perfectionists. They told me they had been utterly cleansed from sin; every Christian should claim this blessing, and be filled with the Spirit. I found it both impossible to talk to them and most difficult to shake them off. When finally they left me, they pronounced over me the most fearful anathemas. The divine authority such people claim outweighs the possibility of their accepting any human reasoning or influence.

Shrewd and well-balanced people are not likely to fall into these errors, or anything approaching them. But it is important to be warned. Others, without meaning to, have been ensnared by them, despite the best will in the world. We must be alert to these dangers.

Scripture itself equips us with tests to use. In the 4th chapter of his first Epistle John counsels us to test the spirits, whether they be of God. Not all the forces that would invade the soul come from Him: but all these forces whether God-given or not, reach us through the door of the inner self. This counsel, then, is of utmost importance. Try these forces. See if they conform to all that we know of Christ. This provides a sure test.

We gratefully recall that our Lord has provided us with a safeguard. Concerning false prophets He said, "By their fruits you shall know them." The test applies to more than false prophets. Ideas and inspirations must be examined on the strength of the results to which they lead. Is this fruit really of God?

We thus check the word coming to us within with what we know of the Word made flesh. The incarnational revelation in Jesus stands now in the midst of history as the great touchstone of all time. By means of this the "subjective" element is to be tested by the "objective". *That* is something which has not happened *in* us. It has happened *for* us. It has not happened *within* us, but in God's great outer world of time and space. The Christian has His everlasting standard. It is not a rigid, dead thing: it has to do with the living Christ, whose revelation is inexhaustible and with whom is Eternal Life.

It is in this way that like Sibelius we can express the music stirring within us. It answers to the glory that we see in Christ and rises in response to God's objective world around. The inspiration that comes from within is to be tested by, and to find its standards in all that we know of Christ objectively, as we read of Him and come to know Him more and more within the community of His people. These are the safeguards, and they are most necessary.

God in His infinite wisdom and understanding has granted guidance and help to every seeker. The man of whom Isaiah speaks—the wayfaring man, though a fool —can walk into the farthest reaches and the deepest distances of these paths with complete safety. For he has the guidance and companionship of the Lord Himself. To this, however, he must attend constantly. The Bible is his anchor.

After these warning paragraphs we are now the better equipped to see where the highway leads. I have dwelt on these safeguards because in the final chapter we deal with the goal of every true seeker. Before anyone embarks on an adventure he must be thoroughly prepared, especially so when the venture is towards Him who is the source of all life. Undeterred and unafraid we can now realise the splendours and possibilities set before us.

17

The Invasion of the Spirit

A Christian is a person energized in secret for life in the open world.

W. RUSSELL MALTBY [1]

NOW we come to the climax of our study of the Stranger Within, able to envisage something of the possibilities open to us in God through the gateway of the inner self. We shall be thinking about the third person of the Trinity, and the invasion of the Spirit.

I would like to introduce what I want to say by referring to a story told of a most independent youth of five. "Say A", said his teacher, pointing to the letter on the blackboard. "I won't," he replied, "for if I say A you'll go on to make me say B." Very early this child had learned the force of logical and inevitable connection.

It is as if we have been saying A and must now pass on to B. We have thought of the development of our inner nature, of the seed-bed of personality, of the place of communion within the self, and have seen how the forces of life pour in and pour through the inner self, resulting in bodily, mental and spiritual well-being. We have talked together concerning stops and barriers that can arise as obstacles to the flow of these life-giving powers. We have looked, also, at some of the appalling mistakes that people can make as they venture on the life of the Spirit if they forget God. Now we must travel, by the force of logic, and because this is the right sequence, on to B. Whilst all life's forces are ultimately God-given, there are unique, spiritual gifts which God shares with those whose inner being is receptive. In spite of all hazards a clear goal shines before us. On our part it involves nothing less than a basic dedication to the highest good—a complete expression of Jesus in human terms.

In order that we may think adequately we must refer again to the Bible. I believe it is important to notice that in the part of the Old Testament coming from the most primitive sources much is made of the idea of "blessing". To many people this has become almost a cant word, with no clear meaning. Vaguely we speak of "God's blessing", and the phrase is a blanket expression in which thought is lost in a woolly mist. By it I suppose we mean something to do with God's benign regard and munificence: and when we ask for God's blessing on others we desire that something of this may be granted to them.

This word, however, once had quite definite edges. To the ancient Hebrew it was a word of power. Only later did it deteriorate into the arch expression of vague religiosity. In Israel's early days *berakha* meant strength implanted in the personality. By means of the blessing one's inner life was renewed and fortified. When God blessed a man his inner life became resilient, strong, full of courage; and because of this inner reinforcement his outward circumstances improved. He became a source of good counsel—that item of prime importance in those far-off days.

You remember how, in the Genesis account, God "blessed" the things that He had made, and said unto them "Be fruitful, and multiply". The creative power of fecundity was implanted by this "blessing".

So far as God's blessing was experienced by an individual it meant cumulative power. Whilst God was with him, inner strength developed, and outward prosperity consequently followed. Only when a man lost the blessing would his inner self wither, and his prosperity decline. The opposite to the blessing was the curse. For anyone under this, life withered in the negative way. The force of this was described many centuries later by Jesus, in words already quoted. "To him that hath shall be given, and he shall have abundance: but from him that hath not shall be taken away that which he hath." When these ideas of blessing and curse are analysed they are much in accord with those we have been examining in the earlier pages of this book.

The Hebrew also knew of God's *ruach*, His Spirit. This came upon a man to make him mighty to do what God commanded. In the graphic phrases of the Old Testament we are told that the Spirit clothed itself with Gideon, came upon Samson, enabled Bezaleel, the craftsman, to do his skilful work for the Tabernacle, fell upon the prophets, inspiring their understanding and giving them wisdom. The *gibbor hayil*, the "mighty man of valour" of the early days, received strength from God to do great exploits in His name.

Summarising these varying endowments Norman Snaith comments, "The *ruach-adonai* is that power of God, descending upon men, by which they are enabled to do that which, in ordinary circumstances, is impossible."

The distinction we are making is important. In passing from the idea of the "blessing" to that of the invasion of the Spirit, we are moving from A to B. All that has gone before in previous chapters could be thought of under the conception of "blessing", the reinforcement of our normal powers, a bestowal by God of divine adjustment. But all this can happen while He Himself is in a sense "remote" from us. In the case of the invasion of the Spirit it is God who works within us, and His work that is being done through us. The empowerment is something out of the ordinary altogether, belonging to the realm of completely supernatural endowment.

When we turn from the Old Testament to the New we notice that the Spirit is associated with Jesus. When granted to His men, it becomes the power of God making these hitherto ineffective disciples into apostles, powerful witnesses to their Lord. The Spirit today, and always, is effective power within a man's nature, and within the life of the world, to take the contents of the Gospel and make them dynamic, full of meaning, effective to deal with each individual's sin, and to renew his inner life. The Spirit brings to remembrance the things which Jesus said and did. The Spirit increasingly extends the significance of all that He is. The Spirit leads men into the Truth: indeed He *is* the Spirit of Truth (i.e. of absolute reality). This is what the New Testament itself says about the Spirit.

We need to notice, too, that in the days when Jesus lived in Galilee, and walked the streets of Jerusalem, the Spirit was fully His. In the Synagogue at Nazareth He read from Isaiah, "The Spirit of the Lord is upon me, because he hath anointed me to preach the gospel to the poor . . . to preach deliverance to the captives, and recovering of sight to the blind . . ." "This day," said Jesus, "is this scripture fulfilled in your ears." He Himself was certain that the Spirit was investing Him with power to do the work to which God had ordained Him.

Finally the Spirit invaded His disciples, equipping them for their work, too. Through the Spirit they now knew the living force of the great Gospel events and this, first of all, for themselves. Not only were they witnesses of the facts of Christ's life: but to the power of these events to revolutionize men's natures.

At Pentecost the coming of the Spirit was given an historic setting. The event was unique, definite, and unforgettable. None of the men waiting in prayer that day in the Upper Room could ever overlook what happened. A Power burst upon them, and within them. They had been waiting, as Jesus had commanded, for "the promise of the Father of which you have heard through me". The promise was now fulfilled. In the city, where only a few weeks before their leader had hung on the gallows, they had been waiting within a close-guarded retreat. Now the Spirit forced them out into the streets, willing and able to explain the source of their extraordinary energy and *joie de vivre*. In making his explanations, Peter was guided to preach the Gospel for the first time. "It is all because of Jesus," he had to say, "whom you, and your leaders crucified." And the Spirit was so much behind the events of Cross and Resurrection announced that day that three thousand souls were added there and then to the Church in Jerusalem.

It is not my intention to pursue the story of the apostolic community under the power of the Spirit. The account is to be read in the Acts of the Apostles. What I want to underline is that these men knew, unmistakably, that power had come upon them. It was an invasion: most certainly an "extra" power: and it was of God. By means of it weak men were made strong. As the Lord had promised, they were able to witness before kings and governors. By the Spirit's inspiration they did the things they were previously powerless to accomplish. "And greater things shall ye do," our Lord had said to them in days when they could scarce credit it, "because I go to the Father."

The all-important question is, where did this invasion happen? I am not referring to the location of the Upper Room, but the place where it happened individually for these men. The answer is clear: it took place within their inner nature, prepared and receptive.

To stress this point we need only instance the case of Peter.[2] Before the Cross, this man was an intensely committed disciple. When he said, "I'll go to the death for you," and "Though all forsake thee, yet will not I," Peter meant what he was saying. He believed it completely with all he knew of himself. To use modern terminology he meant it with the full force of his conscious mind. Jesus tried to tell this rugged man the truth about himself, and what he would do. But Peter would not have it. Then the dramatic events of the Passion burst upon him, ploughing up the very depths of his nature. When it was over, he knew himself for what he was and understood better what his Lord meant to him. In answer to the three-times repeated question, Lovest thou me? he said, "Lord thou knowest all things, Thou knowest that I love thee." Here is a humbled Peter, made ready to receive the gift Jesus promises to those who will wait in humble and expectant faith.

At Pentecost, it happened. Peter, and the others, were invaded at a deeper level than they had previously known. Commitment and discipleship became something reaching every fibre of their being. To them, willing and waiting, the Spirit came. The result was new men and a new Peter, now really the Rock. After this event we read of the rulers of Israel, "They marvelled at the boldness of Peter and John, and took knowledge of them that they had been with Jesus."

Only after a survey of this kind are we likely to realise the gap between the power the disciples knew and the kind of thing we sometimes sing about in church. On the first Whit Sunday, a hurricane was blowing in the Upper Room, not a gentle breeze. The invasion of the Spirit heralded a new dimension of Christian experience. If the word "blessing" has become devalued, so, most tragically, has the conception and understanding of the power of the Holy Spirit.

> *Softer than gale at morning prime*
> *Hovered His holy Dove.*[3]

are words affording a most inadequate picture of Pentecost.

Now there are several points to be noted regarding this invasion. It is of such a character that the gift is not likely to be known in the early stages of Christian experience. I know that this assumption is made—it was made on the

Day of Pentecost. "The gift is to you and your children," announced Peter, and also to those who "believed". No doubt this was so, in a measure, but not in its fulness. This kind of language would be used because the Jews traditionally associated the outpouring of God's Spirit upon all flesh with the coming of the Messiah—as the prophecy from Joel quoted by Peter indicates.

Spiritual gifts come to people in such varying fashion that it is always a mistake to dogmatise. What I would say, however, is that it is possible to know contact with God, to accept His forgiveness, to feel His touch upon our lives, without knowing this fulness of power. Far too many assume that the lower reaches of the Christian faith are all that are available, or necessary. "This is all that I have known," they say to themselves, "therefore this is all that there is to know." Reasoning like this, some Christians assume either that New Testament language about the Spirit is exaggerated, or else that "the New Testament era was exceptional", the implication being that the Spirit no longer visits men in quite the same way.

Events however belie this. One meets with men and women whose endowment is so obviously of God. What they show is not a reinforcement of ordinary human attributes, but a God-given invasion of their natures. Power is radiated. When I met C. F. Andrews I knew I was meeting a person of this calibre. There have been others, some working in very humble and obscure ways. Their lives have an added quality, and their "witness" to their Lord is both winsome and powerful.

These are the lives that beckon us: lives like that of Francis, the adventurer who became a saint: Augustine, the libertine who became a Church leader. A power is to be seen expressing itself through people of this kind that witnesses to its origin. Men as different as Studd, the England cricketer turned evangelist, Cheshire the bomber V.C. now saving lives with his homes throughout the world,

Starr Daily, recidivist and criminal now writing and teaching in the name of Christ, Gladys Aylward the servant girl become world missionary—these and thousands like them witness to a God-given power entering their lives at a deep level and enabling them to serve in an altogether new way. "I was like this," they can say, "and now He has invaded my life." They offer no other explanation of the basic change that has overtaken them. It is all of God. It must be. Without Him human nature reverts to type.

Here is the answer to those who say—as some have said to me—that they do not understand what is meant by such phrases as "Christ in you". The Spirit, as the New Testament makes clear, delights above all else to recreate Christ within those who have faith in Him. God's ambition, it could be said, is to see Christ being "formed again" in thousands upon thousands of people. This is the "inward Christ" who transforms our nature from the centre. We continue to be unique personalities with our special traits, idiosyncracies, and interests. But through us all Christ begins to shine. We have this deep unity in Him.

Paul, writing to a group of early Christians in the Roman province of Galatia, tells them how earnestly he waits for God's processes in them to go forward "until Christ be formed in you".

It is worth noticing that this basic change is often evidenced in the embracing of a form of service hitherto viewed with disfavour. Some of us in the ministry would have to say that such a career was not in our minds at one time. If anyone had suggested it we should have thought they were making a joke in very bad taste.

I have known girls who vowed that the one thing they would never do would be to become a nurse, or teach in a school, who, when God's Spirit has gripped them, discovered a vocation in these very directions. They have entered into these callings with relish and great success.

Christ in them has prompted not only new motivations, but has made possible a new way of living.

Ida Scudder grew up in India as the daughter of medical missionaries. The one thing she vowed she would never be was a medical missionary, and the place to which she would never return was India. Her lasting monument is in the hospital at Vellore. Her name will be remembered as long as missionary annals last. And as to the quality of her witness, the remark of one Indian woman will suffice, "I cannot see your Jesus, but when I see our doctor mamma, I think I see Him."

It is not often that a man gives up a university appointment to take up the humdrum work of a country minister. Professor E. Keri Evans did. His life, he tells us, passed through three phases: the first when with all the ardour of youth he pursued the *Beautiful,* and became no inconsiderable poet. The second was when he turned philosopher, enjoying a fellowship at Glasgow, under Caird, and then becoming Professor at Bangor. At this stage, he tells us, he was earnestly seeking the *True.* Finally, as a result of the way God opened for him, he entered a third stage, combining all for which he had been seeking under the spell of the other two, but adding now the dimensions of the *Good* and the *Holy.*

It was after he began his work as a minister that he came to know the breath of the Spirit. One afternoon in a convention meeting, he accepted Christ as Lord in a deeper way than ever before. He felt his pride in his achievements, the honour and position his academic life had brought him, shrink into nothingness. He was liberated. It was, he says, "as though there was the sound of a new harmony in my subconscious". A further tide of this experience came when he returned home and prayed that God would deal with one of his greatest weaknesses—irritability and bad temper. In that moment, he reports, "I was baptised with streams of life-giving, cleansing, transforming power for about half an hour that made me feel clean and healthy and joyous to the very depths of my being." So this erstwhile Professor of Philosophy found himself able to stand by the wheelwright, the ploughboy, the factory-worker, the housewife, the needy and the dying as a man with a word to them from God, a man bringing a sense of the Presence. "The interest of teaching theories about Christ to students," he comments, "paled beside the interest of teaching Christ to reborn young people."[4]

One has seen this miracle repeated in different ways many times. Folk who thought of Christianity as a philosophy, or a way of life, have come to know it as an invading force. People have been swung into a new path of service for Christ, and been equipped by His Spirit to do it.

The great refrain of their experience is the word "within". What was previously known in external fashion has become a living power in their inner nature. Let the writer of the *Confessions* speak for the others. It was at the age of thirty-three that Augustine knew this invasion, and it was something which deepened and developed from that time onwards. Reading his book carefully you will notice the significance of words like "inward" and "within". "Thou wert more inward to me than my most inward part," he writes. God had become "the life of my life".

There are some things which cannot happen until all is prepared. It is so with the coming of the Spirit. God wants to cast this Fire upon the earth: but He must wait until lives are expectant and ready.

How great is the work of preparation, with the Spirit always guiding, influencing persuasively, waiting patiently, lovingly as the years slip by. How often *afterwards* we wish we had surrendered earlier. If we are eager we shall be led to the place where this can happen. So many of us have an ingrained egotism which must first be overcome. Pride and self-will block the spiritual potentials. But God will always help us if we will but let Him. In prayer He will show us the way. Some of us are so obstinate that it is only after quite needless personal suffering that we come to know our innermost need. But if we are sincere and patient the time *will* come.

Prepared, and ready. Then, while we wait, the Fire descends. The power that visits us is for His glory only. May He save us from ever supposing that any honour is due to us. We are but servants, yet true sons and daughters in His world family, able to serve in the power of the Spirit according to the great example of Jesus our Saviour.

At last the goal of God's desiring for each of us is reached. We are transformed within, in the place where God is able to reveal His Son afresh, so that something of His matchless life begins to glow behind the lineaments of our own. This is the possibility and the invitation. The choice is ours.

God, who in Jesus visited the earth and continues to come in the power carrying forward all that Christ "began both to do and to teach", invites us to share in His continuing story.

Surely, there can be only one answer.

With this in mind, then, I kneel in prayer to the Father, from whom every family in heaven and on earth takes its name, that out of the treasures of his glory He may grant you strength and power through his Spirit in your inner being, that through faith Christ may dwell in your hearts in love. With deep roots and firm foundations, may you be strong to grasp, with all God's people, what is the breadth and length and height and depth of the love of Christ, and to know it, though it is beyond knowledge. So may you attain to fullness of being, the fullness of God himself. (Eph. 3: 14–19 N.E.B.)

A PRAYER OF ST. FRANCIS

Lord, make me a channel of Thy Peace
That where there is hatred—I may bring love,
That where there is wrong—I may bring the spirit of
*   forgiveness,*
That where there is discord—I may bring harmony,
That where there is error—I may bring truth,
That where there is doubt—I may bring faith,
That where there is despair—I may bring hope,
That where there are shadows—I may bring Thy Light,
That where there is sadness—I may bring Joy.

Lord, grant that I may seek rather
To comfort—than to be comforted;
To understand—than to be understood;
To love—than to be loved;

For it is by giving—that one receives;
It is by self-forgetting—that one finds;
It is by forgiving—that one is forgiven;
It is by dying—that one awakens to eternal life.

                              Amen.

NOTES

Chapter 1—LOOK WITHIN!

[1] Luke 17: 21. This seems the inevitable quotation with which to begin, though we must not make the mistake of claiming too much for it. The Greek *entos humòn* could mean either "within you" or "among you", and scholars have wrangled endlessly as to which is the true meaning. Linguistically either is possible. What we really need to know is what Jesus said in His native Aramaic.

[2] Actually these are the words of D. C. Somervell on p. 217 of his *Abridgement* of Vols. I–VI of *The Study of History* (O.U.P.). Toynbee's own sentence reads "makes it possible for the personality to realise individual potentialities which might have remained in abeyance if the individual in whom they were immanent had not been released for a moment from his social toils and trammels." (*The Study of History*, Vol. 3, p. 248, O.U.P.)

[3] *Meditations* 4: 3, 7: 59, 10: 38 (the latter is a very free translation).

Chapter 2—ALARM BELLS

[1] *Poems:* "Dover Beach".

[2] *Human Destiny:* Longmans, Green & Co., 1947, New York and London.

[3] *ibid*, p. 267, quoted by permission of Longmans, Green & Co. both in New York and London. The first sentence of the preamble to the constitution of UNESCO contains these words, "since wars begin in the minds of men, it is in the minds of men that the defence of peace must be constructed."

[4] Books like William H. Whyte's *The Organisation Man* and David Riesman's *The Lonely Crowd* help us to be aware of some of the dangers.

Chapter 3—THE SEED-BED OF PERSONALITY

[1] *Collected Poems:* "The Everlasting Mercy".

[2] For an exposition of some of the dangers of modern advertising see Vance Packard's *The Hidden Persuaders*.

[3] *The Life of Francis Thompson:* Everard Meynell: Burns and Oates Ltd., pp. 46, 49; quoted by permission.

Chapter 4—POWER WITHIN

[1] *Essays:* "The Over-Soul".

Chapter 5—CREATIVE FORCES

[1] *A Testament of Devotion.*

[2] See e.g. *The Devotions of Saint Anselm* ed. C. C. J. Webb, Methuen & Co. The *Proslogion* is included and begins with Anselm's account of how he came to write it.

[3] *So Long to Learn:* Heinemann, pp. 185ff.

[4] The quotations from *The Everlasting Mercy* and *So Long to Learn* are by permission of The Society of Authors, Dr. John Masefield, O.M. and Messrs. Macmillan of New York.

[5] Quoted from *Bertrand Russell: The Passionate Sceptic:* Alan Wood: George Allen & Unwin Ltd., p. 50; by permission.

Chapter 6—EVERY IDLE WORD

[1] *Leaves of Grass:* "When I read the book".

[2] Towards the beginning of the century, the Viennese psychiatrist Sigmund Freud, whose theories and writings have shocked many people, issued a book which proved to be one of his most popular. In it he turned from the study of abnormal minds to reveal something of the working of the normal mind. It is called *The Psychopathology of Every-day Life*, and in it he investigates just this kind of situation.

[3] These words are, of course, a paraphrase of what is given in the versions. See page 148 later for further comments on Peter's story.

[4] *Fight against Fears:* Lucy Freeman: Gollancz, London.

Chapter 7—A PLACE OF COMMUNION

[1] *The Gate of the Year: A Book of Poems* "Moving Inwards to God".

[2] Charlotte Perkins Gilman.

[3] Saul Kane in Masefield's *The Everlasting Mercy*: the italics are mine.

[4] This fact explains the confusion in the accounts. In Acts 9: 7 the men with Paul heard the voice; in Acts 22: 9 they saw the light but heard not the voice. The truth would seem to be that everything that happened, happened to Paul, and the others shared in it only by means of his explanations.

[5] Gerhard Tersteegen.

Chapter 8—THE WAY FORWARD

[1] The hymn "Talk with us, Lord, Thyself reveal".

[2] *The Invading Gospel:* Geoffrey Bles 1958: quoted by kind permission.

[3] See e.g. John 5: 19, 30; 8: 28f; 12: 49f; 14: 10.

Chapter 9—STEPS IN PRAYER

[1] I have been unable to locate this quotation, which I noted some time ago.

[2] The books on Prayer worthy of recommendation are legion. The reader might find great help in Dr. Glenn Clark's *I will lift up mine eyes* (Arthur James Ltd., Evesham). The author has a book entitled *Secrets of Answered Prayer* (from the same publisher).

[3] Available from the Epworth Press, London. An even better introduction to private habits of devotion is found in Dr. Weatherhead's recent book *A Private House of Prayer* (Hodder and Stoughton, London and Abingdon-Cokesbury, New York).

[4] *George Washington Carver:* Rackham Holt, Phoenix House, London, p. 268: quoted by permission.

Chapter 10—BY FAITH WE LIVE

[1] *Man for Himself.*

[2] *Faith in the Synoptic Gospels: A Problem in the Correlation of Scripture and Theology:* Fr. Edward D. O'Connor, C.S.C., University of Notre Dame Press, Notre Dame, Indiana.

[3] *On to Orthodoxy:* first published in 1939 by Hodder and Stoughton, London.

[4] *In Search of Myself:* Geoffrey Bles Ltd. 1961.

[5] Martin Luther's hymn *Aus tiefer Noth schrei ich zu dir* is in the English translation by Catherine Winkworth.

Chapter 11—RICHER LIVING

[1] *Poems.*

[2] The reference is to pp. 145ff of *The Lonely Heart.*

[3] They are recounted in *Body, Mind and Spirit:* Worcester and McComb: Hodder and Stoughton, and Charles Scribner's Sons, pp. 201–5.

Chapter 12—OUR OUTGOING INFLUENCE

[1] *Leaves of Grass:* "Song of the Open Road".

[2] Edward Caird, Master of Balliol's description of one of his tutors, Sir John Conroy.

[3] And the heart, typically, was the centre of *thought*, e.g. "As a man thinketh in his heart so is he."

Chapter 13—LOVE IS THE KEY

[1] *Poems: Some Feasts and Fasts:* "A Song for the least of all saints".

[2] This quotation is also from *Man for Himself.* The italics here are mine.

[3] Colossians 3: 14 N.E.B.

Chapter 14—HEALTH AND HEALING

[1] Paracelsus was a Swiss physician whose real name was Theophrastus Bombastus von Hohenheim. He lived from 1493 to 1541 and was deeply interested in mysticism.

Chapter 15—RELEASE

[1] *Towards Fidelity.*
[2] In his book *Rediscovering Prayer.*

Chapter 16—SAFEGUARDS

[1] *The Imitation of Christ.*
[2] Republished 1934 under the title *Group Movements of the Past and Experiments in Guidance*: Faber and Faber.
[3] *ibid*, p. 157, by permission of Messrs. Faber and Faber.

Chapter 17—THE INVASION OF THE SPIRIT

[1] From an address by the late Rev. Dr. W. Russell Maltby, a former President of the British Methodist Conference.
[2] We have referred before to Peter's story (see p. 57).
[3] e.g. John Keble's hymn (in other ways so excellent) "When God of old came down from heaven".
[4] These extracts are from *My Spiritual Pilgrimage: From Philosophy to Faith* by E. Keri Evans, translated from the Welsh by T. Glyn Thomas, published 1961 by James Clarke & Co. Ltd.: by the publisher's kind permission.

AUTHOR'S NOTE

I have been most careful to acknowledge indebtedness to authors and publishers, but should I have omitted any acknowledgment of this kind, I would be glad if my attention could be drawn to it, and I will rectify the omission in the reprint.